Pinstripe Defection

Pinstripe Defection

A Small-Town Attorney's

Battle with the New York Yankees

Clay McKinney

To Lauren and Emily

Life will always be what you make it.

-Clay McKinney

To my son and best friend, Colin.

The world is yours so never be afraid to pursue your passion.

-Jason Browning

Pinstripe Defection
A Small Town Attorney's Battle with the New York
Yankees

Copyright © 2010 by Clay McKinney

For contact information please visit:
www.pinstripedefection.com

Cover design by Clay McKinney
Cover artwork used with permission from iStock
Author photo by Brian McMahen

First Edition
ISBN 978-0-615-41655-7

Pinstripe Defection

"Because it was a lot of unlegal stuff that was out there that I didn't want to get in to, like sitting here right now. We did a lot of unlegal stuff. It was not proper and when things like that come out, it's not healthy for the New York Yankees or for Major League Baseball… and also for me."
- Jorge Oquendo, former New York Yankees scout

At the age of three, Jason Browning picked up a bat and ball and was immediately electrified. The game of baseball grabbed him and he never had to be pressured to play by his parents, friends or future coaches. Even at a young age, he remembered playing at his mother's home in Arlington, Texas, where second base was his father's blue van, parked at the curb across the yard from the front porch, which served as home base. First and third bases became whatever spot Jason chose for any particular game. He would grip his shiny red plastic bat and stand before his father, who lobbed balls over and over until Jason swung for a hit and raced toward the imaginary first base, then to the van's tire for second, on to the imaginary third base, and finally home, touching the welcome mat on the porch. On lucky days when the Texas Rangers played at their stadium a few blocks away, Jason ran his own diamond to the roar of the crowd.

For years he participated in the sport every way he could, even becoming a registered agent with the Major League Baseball Players Association after he graduated law school. In 2002 he was a young attorney, only twenty-nine-years-old, when he met a Mexican League team owner, Señor Gustavo

Pinstripe Defection

Ricalde, whose problems hinted at the competitive and often controversial world of international baseball scouting, specifically Cubans. Once these players signed, their ascent to the major leagues was often a crawl through mazes of language barriers, cultural misunderstandings, and opportunistic— sometimes corrupt—agents, scouts and representatives. But it was an unfulfilled contract, at the very least, that prompted Sr. Ricalde to ask Jason for help. The New York Yankees, he said, owed money to his team, the Yucatan Lions, because Ricalde had helped scouts from the Yankees sign Michel Hernández, a promising Cuban player. It didn't take long for Jason Browning, small-town attorney and baseball lover, to take on Ricalde's case and knowingly pit himself against one of the most powerful sports teams in the world, the New York Yankees.

"At this moment I am tired to knocking doors in different places, lawyers, immigration offices and the proceedings are at great length with not a fast solution to my serious problem. This must be lack of observation, patience and serenity of all responsible parties. I am a Cuban baseball player, that only was looking for freedom and on baseball I saw that opportunity, and now I feel a slave of the New York Yankees..."
- Michel Hernández, in a 1999 letter to Bill Murray, Director of Operations, Major League Baseball

CHAPTER 1

"Winning is the most important thing in my life, after breathing. Breathing first, winning next."
- George M. Steinbrenner, III, owner, New York Yankees (1930-2010)

In December 2002, Major League Baseball held its
Winter Meetings in Nashville, Tennessee, at the Opryland
Hotel. With nearly 3,000 rooms, the Opryland was the largest
non-casino hotel in the world. Even so, the events surrounding
the meetings were so numerous they spilled into the other
nearby venues. Parties, meetings, conferences, and vendor
displays were featured throughout the area surrounding the
Opryland Hotel. Shuttles were provided to usher the attendees
to and from the various events. The never-ending schedule
insured boredom was impossible in Nashville that weekend.

As the Winter Meetings were drawing to a close,
baseball equipment manufacturers stuffed a sports bar for one
off-site party. They had spent the past few days peddling goods
to major and minor league baseball teams worldwide. The reps
gathered at the bar, some to celebrate their sales successes and
others to drink away their failures. Whether they were selling
stadium seats or souvenirs, the reps seemed determined to bring
this year's meeting to a memorable end.

Jason Browning, an attorney from Fort Smith, Arkansas,
and Chris Fanta were in attendance. Chris Fanta, a sports agent
based out of Chicago, knew several of the reps in attendance.
Chris had invited Jason along to get away from the meetings for
a while. Jason was a registered representative with the Major
League Baseball Player's Association and worked regularly
with Chris on player contract issues. Being completely
immersed in baseball for a few days was something Jason
looked forward to every year, and besides, he always enjoyed
hanging out with his friend who shared a love for baseball and

an unusual sense of humor. The Winter Meetings always reminded Jason of his passion for the game, but they were strenuous nonetheless.

Jason and Chris were fighting their way through the tightly packed crowd towards the bar. Finally the two spotted a narrow opening, and Chris wedged in his shoulder to order a round of beer. For the past several minutes Chris' cell phone had been ringing incessantly, but due to the noise surrounding the festivities, the calls went unanswered.

"Here you go," Chris said to Jason as he handed off an opaque pint of Guinness.

The two again fought their way out of the crowd looking for a relatively quiet spot in which to talk. Luckily, Jason had little trouble following Chris, a beacon in the chaos, who stood several inches above the sea of patrons. As they shuffled towards a less crowded corner of the pub, Jason saw Chris look down at his cell phone. Upon reaching a table that was filled with empty beer bottles and drink glasses, Chris pulled his phone from the clip. A sports agent was naked without his cell phone.

"Fuck, that was Eddie. He's called three times in the past five minutes," Chris shouted to Jason above the roar of the revelry, sliding the phone back into its cradle. Eddie Diaz was Chris' partner in the Pro Talent agency.

Jason said, "Shouldn't you call him back?"

"You know Eddie. He panics over everything. If it's that important, he'll call back."

Just as Chris finished the sentence and began to sip his fresh beer, the phone rang again. "Good God," he said as he whipped the phone to his ear, "Eddie, what the hell do you want? You need what?" Chris yelled over the noise of the energetic crowd. "I can barely hear you...Speak up. We're at the rep party... All right, all right, we'll be there as soon as we can."

With a look of annoyance, he shoved his cell back into its place.

"What was that all about?" Jason asked.

"He wants us to meet some guy tonight at the hotel, said it was urgent," Chris responded while rolling his eyes.

Jason tipped his glass of Guinness before replying, "Let's hit it. I'm ready to get out of here anyway."

The two friends, brought together by their passion for baseball, took the time to finish their beverages before fighting the crowd a final time. They stepped from the smoke-filled pub into the brisk December night, both breathing in a lung full of fresh air.

The last of the arriving passengers filed from the shuttle as they waited for a chance to board. The two settled into a bench seat near the front and waited for the remainder of the shuttle to fill with booze-soaked party goers returning to the Opryland Hotel. Along the way, laughter erupted from time to time as the two shared stories and the occasional joke.

If Jason and Chris were hoping for salvation from the masses, the hotel was not the place. It was still bustling with attendees of the Winter Meetings. Even at an hour before midnight, things showed no signs of slowing down.

Chris shuffled along with the stream of passengers as he turned to Jason, "I told Eddie I'd call him when we got here." He dialed his partner's number, "Hey man, where are you? It's so crowded I can't see a damn thing…Okay, Okay, we'll meet you there." Chris slapped his cell phone shut in mid-stride, "He wants to meet at the rotating bar."

The rotating bar at the Opryland during the Winter Meetings was the place for the who's who in baseball. Any given night, one could see a variety of baseball players, managers and front-office executives. It was swarming with figures from every baseball lover's dreams. That night Lou Piniella, Chuck Lamar - the Manager and General Manager of the Tampa Bay Devil Rays - and Alan Trammel were among those sipping their cocktails at the bar. Trammel had just recently been hired by the Detroit Tigers to be manager and was celebrating with his colleagues.

Chris and Jason realized they had just traded one crowded bar for another, but this crowd carried much more weight in the world of baseball. For Jason, it somehow made slicing through the horde much more tolerable.

"There he is," Chris blurted as he quickened his pace towards Eddie Diaz.

"Hey, hey," Eddie said with a widening smile.

Greetings were exchanged between Chris and Eddie then Eddie and Jason before the group turned to the fourth man standing just outside their circle.

"Jason, Chris, I would like you to meet Señor Gustavo Ricalde," said Eddie. The men shook hands. "He owns the Yucatan Lions of the Mexican League."

"Pleasure to meet you, sir," Chris said.

Jason added, "Señor Ricalde."

Señor Ricalde was a diminutive but well-built man complete with a very distinguished look. His grey hair and immaculate dress gave the impression of a respected man of industry. Jason soon discovered that Ricalde was respected, not only in the world of business but also in the game of baseball. A self-made millionaire, he had founded a chain of thirteen grocery stores called Super Más in Mexico nearly twenty-five years earlier. His wealth had enabled him to purchase a piece of his dream: his own baseball team.

"Ask him if he wants something to drink," Chris asked, referring to Señor Ricalde.

Eddie, a native of the Dominican Republic, turned to Ricalde to translate the question. "No, he's okay," Eddie responded. "I think this is a bit late for him, but he wanted to meet with Jason before he left. He's got an early flight back to Mexico in the morning."

Jason wondered why it was so urgent to meet this man at such a late hour if he had an early flight and why was Eddie so insistent the two meet?

The group moved to a flowerbed filled with plastic plants near a low brick wall in the lobby surrounding the rotating bar.

Jason, ready to know why Eddie was so eager and ever the curious attorney, jumped in, "So what is the issue here?"

"Señor Ricalde has already told me a little," Eddie responded, "But I'll let him start again."

Jason and Chris, overcome with curiosity, listened intently. As Señor Ricalde talked, Eddie passed along the story. "In 1996, Señor Ricalde was introduced to a young player by the name of Michel Hernández. Hernández was a catcher on the Havana Industrialists team from Cuba until he defected while the team played an exhibition game in Mexico. A friend of Ricalde's got the two men together. At the time, Señor Ricalde had a working relationship with the Yankees, so he called a Yankees scout he knew in Mexico to give him notice of Hernández' defection."

"Who was the scout?" Jason interrupted, already intrigued by the mention of the New York Yankees.

Eddie asked Ricalde before he answered. "His name was Carlos Paz. Paz then contacted Jorge Oquendo, whom he apparently reported to at the time. Oquendo and another man from the Yankees' front office, Gordon Blakeley, flew to Mexico within days to watch the kid work out. That night there was a contract signed between Ricalde and the Yankees."

"What were the terms of the contract?" Jason asked.

"It said that if Hernández ever made the Yankees forty-man roster, they would pay Señor Ricalde half a million dollars."

"Five hundred grand, huh?" Jason said while in deep thought. He knew five hundred thousand dollars was nothing to the Yankees. "If this all happened in 1996, why is he just now talking to us? Why wait so long?"

Eddie spoke to Ricalde and then said, "Not until this past fall did Hernández finally make the Yankees forty-man roster."

"What does he want me to do?" Jason asked.

"He wants you to send a letter to the Yankees. Apparently, they have not held their end of the deal."

Jason sat back in shock. He could not believe that this man, whom he had just met, wanted him to draft a half-million-dollar demand letter to the New York Yankees! Questions were flying through his head. He needed a lot more information before he could consider doing such a thing.

"I've got several questions," Jason said.

"Later," Eddie said. "Señor Ricalde said that he has got to get to bed. I'll help you get all the information you need after he gets back to Mexico."

Jason was a stickler for detail, intense, and not knowing the full story left him unsatisfied.

Nevertheless, Jason, Eddie and Chris said their goodbyes to Señor Ricalde before he retired for the evening. The three stayed there to further discuss the case.

Jason strolled to the bar for another beer. Along the way he muttered under his breath, "A demand letter to the New York Yankees. Right! This isn't going to get very far." Yet Jason took his potential client seriously. Ricalde, through his soft-spoken manner, came across as a genuine and honest person. Though sending the letter to the Yankees seemed ludicrous at first glance, Jason felt there might just be something to Ricalde's claim.

Upon returning, Jason handed each of his friends another beer and sat down. The seemingly ridiculous request from Ricalde was still ringing in his head. Before he could begin listing aloud the numerous reasons why he should not take this case, Eddie revived the conversation.

"You know, Oquendo is here," Eddie said, referring to the former Yankees' scout who met with Señor Ricalde.

Jason's face lit up, "Really? Hell, if we could find him…I would love to see what he has to say about all of this."

Eddie drew closer to Jason. With his face inches away, Eddie said, "Man, do you realize how big this could be for you? Shit, it's the New York Yankees!"

Dismissing the significance Eddie attributed to the issue, Jason realized that there were about a thousand questions he'd have to get answers to before he went anywhere near the Yankees office. "Let's start by finding Oquendo."

Their efforts to locate Jorge Oquendo at the meetings were unsuccessful, and eventually the three said their goodbyes and went to their respective rooms. Later Jason found out that Señor Ricalde had already encountered Oquendo earlier in one of the meetings. They would soon learn that Oquendo was the person who signed the contract on behalf of the New York Yankees, and Oquendo's conversation with Ricalde gave him an opportunity to alert his powerful former employers to what was about to unfold.

*   *   *

Baseball is considered an American sport, but baseball in America only predates the establishment of the sport in Cuba by a mere few years. The sport was brought to the island in the mid-1860's in two separate ways. American sailors anchored in Cuban ports taught the sugar-loading native workers how to play the game. Around the same time, Nemisio Guillo, a well-to-do Cuban, brought home a baseball and bat from Mobile, Alabama, where he was in school. The popularity of the sport soon exploded on the island.

In 1869, baseball was banned in Cuba by their Spanish rulers. The Spanish wanted the Cubans to embrace bull fighting, but the Cubans found the sport to be too brutal and barbaric. The rebellious citizens continued to play baseball away from the watchful eye of the Spanish. In this way, baseball became synonymous with freedom and liberation to the Cuban people.

In 1878, a mere two years after the Americans started the National League, Cuba started the Professional Baseball League of Cuba. The league began with three teams: Havana, Matanzas and Almendares. The inaugural championship was won by Havana, led by Esteban Bellan, who became the first Cuban to play professional baseball in the United States.

During the early 1890's, Cubans earned the nickname "the apostles of baseball" by introducing baseball to Mexico, Puerto Rico and the Dominican Republic. During the same period, some American players, including the notorious John McGraw, began touring Cuba for exhibition games during the winter. For the next several decades, the American National League sent teams to Cuba for exhibition games with mixed results. The Cubans were becoming a solid force in professional baseball, many times rivaling the Americans.

These winter exhibitions continued until the 1959 Revolution. Prior to this, American players enjoyed earning some extra money and the warmer winter climate in Cuba. All of that came to an end when Fidel Castro took over the government. The new Cuban government likened professional baseball to exploitation and disbanded the Cuban league in 1962. In its place an amateur league was started. Called the National Series, the new league expanded baseball within Cuba to include some more isolated provinces of the island. This led to true regionalism in Cuban baseball. The locals were rabidly devoted to their local team. The league grew to sixteen teams, which each played a ninety-game season from November to February followed by an eight-team tournament to decide the championship.

In many ways, the Communist government whittled baseball back down to its essence: a pure sport. It was simply baseball. There were no longer salaries, team owners, or corporate sponsorships, some of the many things that detract from professional sports today. However, as the Communist government gained a stranglehold on Cuba, it wasn't long before these players, playing for little more than pride, began to fix their stare on the United States. Thus began the so-called 'modern era' of Cuban baseball.

Some say the golden years of Cuban baseball were during the 1940's, but others say the 1950's. Either way, the Cubans won the Caribbean Series seven times between 1949 and 1960, along with a gold medal in the Pan American Games in 1951 and 1963. The Cubans' dominance was also showcased in the International Baseball Federation World Cup and more recently in the Olympic games, where the Cuban team has won three gold medals and two silvers since 1992.

The history of Cuban baseball is voluminous. There have been more than 150 Cuban-born players in Major League Baseball throughout the years. These players grew up surrounded by baseball, sometimes playing with a stick and ball of tape in the streets of Cuba. It's a story that has changed very little in the past fifty years. These young Cubans dreamed of playing for their regional teams and lived for the chance of being picked to play for the National Team.

Many close to professional baseball feel we have yet to learn the depth of Cuban baseball talent, as many of those who have chosen to defect to play in the U.S. are older and often past their prime. In essence, the belief is that the most talented stay behind and play for their native country. This belief is evidenced by a 129-0 record for the Cuban team in international play over a ten-year period, beginning in 1987. However, it was during this time that political pressure was building and the dam was about to burst.

Ironically, on the Fourth of July in 1991, a pitcher for the Cuban National Team, Rene Arocha, rocked the baseball world by defecting while his team was playing an exhibition game in the United States. Many in the baseball world felt him to be the third or fourth best pitcher on the Cuban team. Arocha ultimately signed with the St. Louis Cardinals for the sum of

$15,000. He was considered by many to be the first wave in a flood of Cuban players who defected to America.

Approximately eighty Cuban players defected over the next decade. Some of the more notable were Rey Ordonez and Rolando Arrojo. Ordonez defected in 1993 and went on to play shortstop for seven years for the New York Mets. It is said that Ordonez realized his play would be limited in Cuba by the better players in front of him, so he left to pursue a career in the U.S. If Ordonez couldn't start for the Cuban team, many wondered just how much talent was pent-up in the island nation.

Rolando Arrojo, a pitcher, fared much better than his earlier counterpart, Arocha. In 1996, Arrojo signed a contract with the Tampa Bay Devil Rays for $7 million. Arrojo had an immediate impact, starting in the All-Star game a mere two years after his debut.

Perhaps the most notable Cuban player to defect was Orlando "El Duque" Hernández. In 1997, Hernández escaped Cuba by boat, but he was already in his early thirties. Most of his prime playing years were spent playing ball in Cuba, but he had to get out. Ever since his half-brother, Livan, had defected two years earlier, Orlando had been banned from baseball by the Cuban government.

Many of these players not only risked their lives to escape the Communist Cuba, they also risked the lives of their families who remained behind. The Cuban government often took out their frustrations on the family of a defected player.

Orlando Hernández was one of the fortunate few able to get his family out of Cuba.

On October 20, 1998, Hernández' team, the New York Yankees, had just won the World Series. He wanted to have his family with him in the United States, so he wrote a letter to Cardinal O'Connor asking for help. After careful consideration, the Cardinal sent a letter, delivered by a representative, Mario Paredes, directly to Castro asking if the family could be allowed to visit Hernández in America. Castro relented, and with help from U.S. Attorney General Janet Reno and FBI Director Louis Freeh, Hernández' family received the proper clearance to enter the United States.

Cardinal O'Connor made arrangements for Hernández' mother, ex-wife and two daughters to fly to Miami, where they were picked up by George Steinbrenner's private plane and were flown to New York to finally reunite with Hernández. Castro said the family members would be welcomed if they decided to return to Cuba, indirectly saying the Hernández family could stay in the U.S.

Not all baseball players who have defected have gone on to play in the big leagues, but all left in search of a better life. Whether it was simply for themselves or for their entire extended family, these players knew of the possible fortunes waiting for them in the United States. After all, if you added the salary of each and every Cuban League player together, the figure would be less than $70,000 per year total.

CHAPTER 2

"The ballplayer who loses his head, who can't keep his cool, is worse than no ballplayer at all."
– Lou Gehrig

Two weeks after the Winter Meetings, Jason was back home in Fort Smith engrossed in cases unrelated to baseball. He gave little thought to his encounter with Señor Ricalde in Nashville. Christmas was fast approaching, and he wanted to wrap up several pending cases before taking a few days of holiday vacation with his pregnant wife Robin.

Jason barely noticed when his secretary placed a fax on a towering stack of documents next to his computer. He reached over to the stack to retrieve what he thought was the next page of the transcripts from a recent deposition, but instead, drew back the fax written in Spanish. On first glance, the only thing he understood was that the fax came from Eddie Diaz, his sports agent associate from Chicago.

Frustrated, Jason strolled down the hall of his law firm to have a legal secretary translate the fax. Jason returned to his office and sat looking around. Nearly every flat surface held some type of baseball memorabilia. He began collecting autographed bats and balls as a child. One piece of memorabilia that Jason has kept for many years and he continues to display on his desk, is a baseball signed by Rick Honeycutt, among other Texas Rangers. The story of how this came about remains vivid for Jason. Once, a friend of Jason's mother managed to get a baseball used during batting practice, just before a Rangers game against the Detroit Tigers. Jason's father decided to take his son to Rick Honeycutt's house and try to have the ball autographed. The opportunity to meet the major leaguer was too good to pass up.

At the time, Rick was a pitcher for the Rangers and Jason was a huge fan. Escorted by his father, Jason rang the doorbell. It was answered by Rick's wife, an extremely pregnant Mrs. Honeycutt. She explained that Rick was in Los Angeles with the rest of the Rangers, playing the Angels (which Jason admits he should have known). Nonetheless, she asked him to leave the ball with her. She promised Rick would autograph it when he returned from the road trip.

It wasn't but a couple of weeks later that a box came in the mail addressed to Jason at his home in Pampa, Texas. In it was the ball signed by every member of the Rangers team. Rick had passed the ball around the clubhouse for all the players to sign. Jason was ecstatic. Getting something like that done today might be next to impossible.

Engrossed in work, Jason's thoughts were interrupted by a knock on his office door. The fax was returned, complete with the translation. Just as before, it was placed on his desk so as to not disturb him, but this time Jason snatched the papers up immediately.

The top of the first page read "Yucatan Lions." His suspicions were confirmed. The correspondence was related to Señor Ricalde. It was a copy of the contract between Ricalde and the New York Yankees, signed by Jorge Oquendo and Ricalde, dated November 21, 1996. The contract verified the five hundred thousand dollar figure conveyed by Ricalde, but now Jason wanted more. He knew the only other person who would voluntarily verify Señor Ricalde's account of the events surrounding the signing of this contract was Jorge Oquendo.

Eddie had emailed Jason Oquendo's cell phone number a few days before, and later that evening, Jason sat at home in his favorite lounge chair and dialed Oquendo's number. After some brief introductions and small talk, Jason quizzed the scout. "In November 1996, did you travel to Yucatan Mexico to scout Michel Hernández?"

"Yes, I did," Oquendo immediately answered.

"Did you make this trip alone?"

"No, Gordon Blakeley was with me in Mexico. He saw Michel work out also."

"How long were you in Mexico for this trip?"

After a brief pause to reflect, Oquendo answered, "I think it was like a day and a half, maybe two days."

"Okay," Jason said as he carefully crafted his questions. "Both you and Mr. Blakeley were employees of the New York Yankees at the time, correct?"

"That's right."

"After you and Mr. Blakeley determined that the Yankees were interested in acquiring Michel Hernández, what happened next?"

"We signed a contract with Ricalde that said if Michel Hernández ever made the Yankees' forty-man roster, the Yankees would pay him $500,000."

"So there was no money exchanged in Mexico during your visit?" Jason asked.

"No."

"What can you tell me about the contract and the negotiation of the contract?"

"It was real simple. Gordon Blakeley told me to talk with Ricalde about what it would take to get Michel, and we wrote up the contract. I took it to Gordon's room for him to look at, and once he said to go ahead and do it, I took it back downstairs and both me and Ricalde signed it."

"When you say Gordon's room, what do you mean?"

"At the hotel we were staying at. All the negotiations took place at the hotel," Oquendo clarified.

"So what happened after the contract was signed?" Jason continued.

"Gordon called a sports agent, Gus Dominguez, for help to get Michel out of Mexico."

"Why was that?"

"Because Michel was Cuban. He had just defected and had no paperwork, so I guess Gordon knew it was going to be hard to get Michel out of the country."

"Okay, what happened next?"

"The next day we handed Michel off to the people who were going to get him out, and after that I left to come home."

After a few more minutes of follow-up questions, Jason began to feel a little more at ease about the situation. Having been asked to represent Ricalde and his Yucatan Lions team without any knowledge of the key witnesses, much less the key facts, Jason likened his initial investigation to assembling a puzzle. It just so happened that the pieces were provided by a non-English speaking client and a scout who lived in another country whom Jason had never met.

He felt his first conversation with Oquendo went well and that Oquendo was being forthright. There wasn't anything that Oquendo did or said that made Jason believe this transaction never took place or that made him question Oquendo's veracity. The details, conveyed by the emphatic, unwavering scout, were specific enough to assure Jason that he could move forward with the demand letter Ricalde had requested.

Very little was known regarding the details of Michel Hernández' defection from Cuba. Three other players from the Cuban team defected at the same time as Hernández, but the specifics of their defection and the later contact with the Yucatan Lions remain a mystery. Señor Ricalde refused to name the individuals who first put him in contact with Hernández because at least one of these individuals was believed to still live in Cuba. As he would describe later during the grievance, "It would be even mortal for them, because to be involved in a matter such as this, it is a very serious crime in Cuba."

The only certain fact was that Hernández was in Mexico for a game with the Havana Industrialists team. He was a starting catcher at the time. Once Hernández met with this mysterious contact, he began the extensive process that would eventually land him in the United States.

Ultimately, Ricalde seized the chance to deal a young Cuban player to the Yankees. Possibly, Ricalde wished to help a young man in a bad situation find his way to a better life. At the time, Cuban players were a very sought-after commodity, and professional American teams paid millions to relatively unknown players, simply because they were Cuban. Some examples for comparison are the signings of Livan Hernández, Rolando Arroyo and Osvaldo Fernandez in 1996 and 1997. In late 1996, Livan Hernández signed a four-year contract for $4.5 million guaranteed, plus $1.5 million in incentives. Two and a half million of the guaranteed money was a signing bonus. Osvaldo Fernandez, also in 1996, signed a $3.9 million contract, guaranteed, plus incentives. In May 1997, Rolando Arroyo signed a Minor League contract with a seven million dollar bonus. These three Cuban defectors played a premium position – pitcher. Similarly, Michel Hernández played the premium position of catcher. At the time of his defection in 1996, he was subject to the market that was established by Livan Hernández, Osvaldo Fernandez and Orlando Arroyo. Accordingly, the $500,000 value set forth in the agreement between the Yankees and the Yucatan Lions was a bargain.

Hernández' defection spawned a flurry of phone calls. Ricalde phoned Carlos Paz, who served as an area scout for the Yankees within Mexico. Paz immediately contacted Jorge Oquendo, who, at the time, was believed to be the Yankees' Coordinator of Latin American scouting and living in Puerto Rico. In turn, Oquendo called Gordon Blakeley, the Director of International Scouting for the Yankees, who worked from the Yankees' home office in Tampa, Florida. Oquendo and Blakeley quickly made arrangements to travel to Mexico to meet with Hernández and assess his talent.

Oquendo was the first to arrive in Mexico in early November 1996. He was already at the Yucatan Lions' stadium with Michel Hernández when Carlos Paz picked up Blakeley from the airport and delivered him to the facility. Paz participated in the workout for Hernández while Blakeley and Oquendo studied the young player. Hernández was tested on his defensive and throwing abilities, as well as his hitting.

After the Yankees' representatives determined that they wanted Hernández, they negotiated and signed a contract with Ricalde that gave the Yankees the rights to Hernández. Three days later, Blakeley made arrangements to fly the young player to Mexico City, where he was turned over to Ken Dominguez, a minor league manager in the Yankees' organization in the Gulf Coast League. Since Hernández did not have the proper documentation, he used the name of Ken's cousin, Juan Dominguez, during this transfer, and Ken Dominguez, fluent in Spanish, would oversee the last part of Hernández' journey. In Mexico City, Hernández was given the paperwork necessary to get him out of the country.

To help with the logistics of getting Hernandez out of Mexico, Blakeley claimed to contact two sports agents who specialized in helping Cuban players through the citizenship process in countries other than Cuba, so the players could then travel to the U.S. The agent ultimately used by Blakeley was Gus Dominguez. (No relation to Ken). Supposedly, Blakeley contacted another agent, Joe Cubas, who was known throughout baseball as an agent who actively aided Cuban players.

Cubas, an American-born son of Cuban immigrants, escaped the island shortly after the revolution in the late 1950's. He received his business degree from Florida International University and worked for his father-in-law in the construction business before he took a job with a friend in a sports-marketing business. Cubas quickly gained a reputation as a big-time broker of Cuban baseball players.

Since then he engineered the signing of dozens of Cuban players in the United States, including Orlando "El Duque" Hernández, the most notable of his clients, who in 1998 penned a $6.6 million, four-year contract with the Yankees. Other key players he helped included Livan Hernández (El Duque's half-brother), Osvaldo Fernandez and Rolando Arrojo.

In Cuba, Cubas had been called a variety of despicable names by sports ministry officials and others. These comments only served to make Cubas somewhat of a cult figure in Miami and other areas with a high population of Cubans, even among those who did not follow professional baseball. Cubas' own cousin and former business associate, Juan Ignacio Hernández Nodar, was sentenced to fifteen years in a Cuban prison after he was caught trying to help players defect.

"The Cuban exiles who hate Castro look at me and my business and say, 'Good, he's making Castro look stupid by taking away one of his major propaganda tools' -- some of the good baseball players in Cuba," Cubas is quoted as saying. "If that happens, it happens. But it's first a business for me, and I like being involved in a love -- baseball. And then comes the element of helping people gain freedom and seek their dream of playing major league baseball. I say, 'In America, you have opportunity, not restraints like in Cuba.' When I'm sitting and talking to them about what life in America can be like, I equate it to baseball. I say, it's like you're up to bat. You can now hit the ball as far as you like. It's beautiful."

Cubas had many detractors, not only in Cuba, but also in the United States. Many accused him of only coming to the aid of the baseball players within the multitude of groups that defected from their homeland. Once in the Bahamas, Cuban defectors rioted when they discovered Cubas was only interested in the baseball players among a particular group. Eventually Cubas secured shipments of food and medicine for the escapees and sought visas for each of the disgruntled from the Costa Rican government.

       *   *   *

Feeling more comfortable after what he had learned from Oquendo, Jason drafted a letter as a representative of the Yucatan club, and on January 3, 2003, the correspondence was sent to Brian Cashman, the General Manager of the New York Yankees. Jason was fairly certain Cashman knew nothing of the deal struck between the Yankees and Yucatan since he was not the General Manager in 1996, but he wanted to start in the upper echelon of the Yankees' management and ensure that the inquiry was directed to the appropriate personnel. The letter summarized the particulars of the contract and demanded payment to fulfill the Yankees' obligation.

Three weeks passed with no reply, and his hopes for a quick resolution were dashed. While waiting for a response from the Yankees, Jason took the opportunity to notify the office of the Major League Baseball Players Association of his participation in the case. He felt compelled to apprise the player's union of this particular grievance although he deemed the case was a 'club versus club' issue and did not directly involve a player. Jason wanted to discuss and resolve any potential or perceived conflicts of interest that might arise because he was a certified player agent but was representing a Mexican League club in a grievance. Because the status of Michel Hernández was not an issue for this specific claim, Jason did not consider his representation of the Yucatan Lions to be a conflict.

Jason contacted Michael Weiner, the General Counsel for the Players Association, to reveal his interest in handling this matter on behalf of Yucatan. Michael asked Jason to summarize the issues in a letter, and he assured Jason that after his review of the issues, he would get back to Jason. In Jason's experience, Michael had always been available to discuss matters and always been quick with a reply to emails or to return phone calls. Feeling there was little else to do until the Yankees and the Players Association responded, Jason turned his attention to the many cases waiting at the office.

Michael Weiner called Jason within days of receiving the letter. Michael said that he would discuss the situation with Gene Orza, the Chief Operating Officer of the Players Association, but that he did not anticipate any problems with Jason's participation in the case. After reassuring Jason again that he could move forward, Michael left Jason with a final bit of advice, "Get it done and get it done quickly." It was sound advice, but as Jason would soon learn, resolving this matter quickly would be virtually impossible.

The following day, Jason was driving home from his office when his cell phone rang.

"Jason, this is Gene Orza."

"Oh, hello Mr. Orza..."

"What are you doing representing a club? You are to represent players only!"

After the initial shock from such a greeting, Jason gathered his composure. "Mr. Orza, I'm an attorney. I represent a lot of different people. Are you saying that just because I am a registered agent of the Players Association that I can't represent hospitals in lawsuits or doctors in malpractice suits either?"

"No, this is different. You are representing a baseball team owner. I tell you what, I'm going to talk with Don Fehr about this and I will get back to you."

When Orza hung up on him, Jason was angry and taken aback. He grew angrier at Orza's subtle threat to call Donald Fehr, the Executive Director of the Players Association. Fehr was a graduate of Indiana University Law School, and early in his career, while in private practice, he worked with Marvin Miller, the first Executive Director of the MLB Players Association in the Andy Messersmith and Dave McNally arbitration case that involved free agency. The case, later known as the Seitz case, after the arbitrator, ultimately lead to the demise of MLB's reserve clause and cleared the way for the current era of free agency.

In 1977, Fehr was hired by his predecessor Marvin Miller as General Counsel for the Players Association. In 1986, the Players Association elected Fehr as Executive Director. Shortly thereafter, he successfully negotiated a settlement in the amount of $280 million for the owners' collusive activities affecting the free agent market in 1987-1988.

Fehr is perhaps best known for his leadership role in the 1994 Major League Baseball Strike. The strike lasted from August 12, 1994 to April 2, 1995 and resulted in the cancellation of over nine hundred games including the 1994 World Series.

Notwithstanding Orza's concerns, Jason believed this to be a club versus club issue; representing Yucatan would in no way compromise any work he would do for players. Though this matter began with a player, Michel Hernández, it was a team, the Yucatan Lions, who sought restitution from the New York Yankees for reneging on a contract for Hernández. Interestingly, but not surprisingly, Jason didn't hear back from Orza or Fehr regarding this issue, so he continued to press forward.

Having grown impatient with the Yankees lack of response, Jason drafted a second letter the first week of February 2003. It was again addressed to Brian Cashman. Jason did not know if the first letter was received or read, but his second letter elicited a response. Apparently, the second inquiry was forwarded to Lonn Trost, General Counsel for the Yankees. Mr. Trost obviously took the letter more seriously. Shortly after receiving the demand, he sent an email to Jason that stated in unequivocal, cold, and direct terms that the Yankees intended to bring this issue to the attention of, not only Kevin Hallinan, the Director of Major League Baseball Security, but also the F.B.I. The Yankees referred to the demand as "ridiculous" and likened the entire case to extortion. The email specifically mentioned Jorge Oquendo and stated that the Yankees would not, at the present time, notify the Cincinnati Reds, Oquendo's current employer, of their employee's ludicrous statements.

Jason found the email curious and wondered why the Yankees would even mention Oquendo's current position or employer. He also thought the Yankees refrained from notifying the Reds because Oquendo was a scout, under contract with that club, and they did not want to potentially interfere with his employment.

Jason's simple demand letter on Ricalde's behalf led to direct threats of notifications to state and federal authorities, including the F.B.I. Jason was not shocked by such responses, laden with unabashed bravado, but he was concerned with the facts surrounding this issue and with Oquendo's job. He knew he must learn every detail surrounding this case. He understood he was combating a seemingly impenetrable force, the New York Yankees.

Without delay, Jason dialed Oquendo's cell phone. Not only did Jason want to warn Oquendo of Trost's threat, but he hoped to find some reassurance. Jason read the email to Oquendo, who merely laughed at Trost's posturing. To Jason's relief, Oquendo seemed completely unfazed by the over-reaching threat. After stifling his laughter, and with a much more serious tone, Oquendo said: "First of all, fuck Lonn Trost and second, you call Trost and tell him, no, beg him to call MLB security. Then tell him that I have already told Lou Melendez, the Vice President of International Baseball Operations, all about this, so the Commissioner's office already knows everything."

Jason couldn't help but chuckle at the comment. But the best news was that the scout from Puerto Rico was not afraid to proceed. Jason sensed Oquendo wanted the truth to be known and apparently wasn't hesitant to face anyone, the MLB or the Yankees. From such a response, Jason had but one thing to do next: contact Lou Melendez. Melendez corroborated Oquendo's story. Oquendo had told the truth. Melendez had been told everything by Oquendo. Melendez told Jason to call Ed Burns, Vice President, Baseball Operations and Administration for Major League Baseball.

Before Melendez hung up, he said, "Even though this is the New York Yankees, half a million dollars is a lot of money."

Jason thought to himself, "Hell, the Yankees make that in beer sales when the Boston Red Sox are in town…midweek!"

Jason did as Melendez suggested and immediately contacted Mr. Burns. After Jason provided a synopsis of the issues, Mr. Burns confirmed that their office had already looked into the issue and agreed that there was enough substantiation to support the filing of a grievance with the Commissioner's office. Jason thought it odd that an investigation had taken place, but he was given the authority to file a grievance. It was as if MLB needed a third party to press the issue further, and Yucatan was that third party. With this blessing, Jason drafted and filed a grievance on behalf of the Yucatan Lions with the office of the Commissioner of Major League Baseball.

Yucatan was a member of the National Association of Professional Baseball Leagues (NAPBL) or the minor leagues, and it had an agreement with MLB wherein the Commissioner would serve as arbitrator for all actions between minor league and major league clubs. The Commissioner's office notified the Yankees of the grievance. Shortly thereafter, a conference call was scheduled between Ed Burns, Jason and the New York Yankees' counsel, Rich Rabin, to discuss the specifics of the grievance. Even placed against the backdrop of Trost's threats, a simple letter to the Commissioner's office served as the genesis of the grievance, one that Jason hoped would be resolved as quickly as it had begun.

Jason was not surprised that the Akin, Gump, Strauss, Hauer & Feld firm would represent the Yankees in this grievance because Randy Levine, President of the New York Yankees, was also a senior attorney at the firm. Rich Rabin was a younger, highly-talented attorney with Akin Gump, a firm with offices at One Bryant Park in New York. The Akin Gump firm was one of the largest law firms in the world, with over one thousand attorneys in fourteen offices scattered around the globe. Rabin held a law degree from Georgetown and was to be the Yankees' lead counsel in the Yucatan case.

Jason anxiously scribbled notes at his desk during the conference call. He hoped the conversation would lead

somewhere, but Rabin was ambiguous and made every attempt
to belittle and stonewall the proceedings. "I don't understand
what the issue is here," Rabin said, in what Jason would learn to
be a typical, obstinate tone. Rabin was a seasoned attorney with
vast experience in employment and labor relations, and Jason
had no doubt he would do a superb job representing the historic
franchise.

"What's there not to understand?" Jason responded.
"The Yankees signed a contract, the stipulations of the contract
have been met and now the Yankees refuse to honor it."

Although no additional threats of pursuing F.B.I.
intervention had been made, Rabin's position was on par with
Trost's previous email. This tone and obtuse approach to the
conference call was merely a glimpse of the Yankees' attitude
that permeated the entire grievance process. Rabin showed how
seriously he was taking the case when he said, "The contract I
received was in Spanish. It hasn't even been translated."

Jason rolled his eyes at the comment. An attorney
charged with defending a grievance against the New York
Yankees would surely have had the contract translated by now,
he thought. Jason had already forwarded the original, un-
translated version of the contract and thought surely, somehow,
the Yankees would have it translated.

The conference call seemed to be going nowhere, but Ed
Burns ended the stalemate by verifying that there was sufficient
evidence to continue the grievance proceedings. He stated that
the parties could begin discovery. This was where the facts of
the case would be disclosed.

Jason knew Rabin must have been furious. Rabin was an intense attorney charged with defending the Yankees, but his counter-part was just as determined, and, given the outcome of the conference call, seemed to be better prepared. Rabin had to be assessing this young attorney from Arkansas and attempting to size him up.

Jason was very encouraged by Ed Burn's acknowledgment that discovery could be conducted because it meant, at a minimum, he would talk to the key witnesses to this transaction and create a factual record for a hearing.

In July 2003, the discovery process began when the Yankees issued a Bill of Particulars to Jason and his client, which asked for specific details regarding the people and events surrounding the case. The Bill of Particulars, a list of written questions asking for details (particulars) about the Yucatan claim, was simply the Yankees' way of discovering the facts surrounding the case. Not only were the Yankees attempting to question the authenticity of the contract by referring to it as the "alleged agreement" within the Bill of Particulars, but they were also beginning to assert that Jorge Oquendo had no authority to sign the contract on behalf of the organization. Jason considered it an attempt by the Yankees to begin to distance themselves from Oquendo, casting some doubt already on the accuracy of the facts as conveyed to Jason.

The case made Jason's competitive juices start to flow. The stubborn determination he held since childhood would serve him well throughout the case. Some attorneys might have taken Trost's threats as warning not to press forward, but

Jason's resolve was never a question, even as a young baseball player.

   *   *   *

  After having moved to Arkansas in the spring of 1987, Jason tried out for the local Boy's Club Babe Ruth team, which held a draft each year. Jason was picked by the Eagle's Lodge team where, at age thirteen, he beat out a fifteen-year-old for the position of second base. This was Jason's first experience on the standard 'adult-sized' baseball field. The ninety feet between the bases, as opposed to the sixty feet base paths in Little League, seemed like miles, but the feel of a real pitching mound really got his attention. He would stand on the mound and stare at the never-ending sixty feet to home plate and marvel that anyone could ever get the ball to the catcher. For him, it was a new game.

  During the first inning of the opening game of the season, Jason reached first base on a single. The next batter sent a groundball to the shortstop. Jason sprinted for second base knowing he was going to be called out, but he wanted to prevent the double play. By going in hard to second, he made it difficult for the defense to turn a double play by throwing out Jason's teammate running to first. Jason slid feet first but his left arm was caught under his body, buckling his forearm under the weight. He knew immediately something was wrong but he refused to come out. He already had one hit - something Jason experienced very few times as he grew older and faced better pitching.

The severity of his injury became readily apparent the next inning when, as second baseman, he caught a ball thrown from the outfield and nearly dropped it because of the excruciating pain. He never said anything to anyone about the pain and eventually finished the game going two for two with two walks.

Later that night Jason described his discomfort to his father who asked about going to the emergency room. Jason refused but got little sleep that night from all the pain. The following morning, just before school, Jason admitted to his father that going to get medical attention was not such a bad idea. X-rays revealed his forearm was actually broken, requiring a cast. His father begged Jason not to tell his mother, who was out of town, that they had not gone to see a doctor the night before. She would be furious. Jason pledged his silence as he didn't see any need to upset his mother, or to subject his dad to a blistering his mom would have surely served up.

As Jason put it, the next few weeks were 'murder' knowing he was missing games. The helpless feeling was unpalatable. Within a few days of the injury he felt fine and didn't understand why he couldn't be back out on the field with his buddies.

The cast was uncomfortable and began to smell. He had had enough. He also had a plan. One day after school, Jason worked with his baseball glove, unsuccessfully trying to fit it over the cast. He resorted to a saw, cutting away pieces of the cast around his thumb and fingers and stopping occasionally to check the size. Feeling as good as he did, he felt there was no

need for the cast anyway. About that time, his father came home
and caught him with the saw in one hand and the glove in the
other. Jason feared the worst. He knew his father was going to
let him have it. After questioning Jason for a moment and
eyeing what damage he had done to the cast, his father said,
"Here, let me help you." He picked up the saw and helped his
son reconfigure the wretched cast. The glove never felt as good.
Nothing could keep Jason from his passion, and of course, the
first thing to do was to try it out. Jason and his father went out
into the yard to play some catch. It worked beautifully. Jason's
plan worked.

The next team practice Jason told the coach that he felt
fine and begged to play. He drove the point home by catching
some balls right in front of the coach. The coach was impressed,
but he was a little fuzzy on whether or not the rules would allow
Jason to play in a game with a cast on. He told Jason that he
would ask the umpire if he could pitch since in that position
Jason was less likely to re-injure the arm.

The next game, the starting pitcher was pulled from the
game and the coach strolled over to the umpire. He explained
Jason's situation and emphasized that there would be no danger
in letting him play from the mound. The umpire agreed and let
the kid with the cast play ball. Even a broken arm did not stand
in the way of Jason's resolve to play ball that season.

CHAPTER 3

"No matter how good you are, you're going to lose one-third of your games. No matter how bad you are you're going to win one-third of your games. It's the other third that makes the difference."

- Tommy Lasorda

Multiple times Jason had spoken to Jorge Oquendo over the phone, but the first time he met Oquendo in person was in July 2003 during the All-Star break in Chicago. The two agreed to meet at some point during the Futures Game. Jason again met up with his friends, sports agents Chris Fanta and Eddie Diaz. They attended the Futures Game on Sunday afternoon at US Cellular Field, formerly Comiskey Park, home of the Chicago White Sox. The Futures Game showcased the top minor league baseball prospects and would be attended by many front office executives.

A few innings into the game, Jason rang Oquendo's cell phone and arranged to meet him near the concession area adjacent to the main gate. When Jason introduced himself, Oquendo looked startled. "My God, you're just a kid." Oquendo said, underneath a lighthearted chuckle.

Not troubled by the statement Jason said, "Listen, we've got to sit down and go over some things. I've got to respond to some questions posed by the Yankees, and I need to make sure I've got everything right."

If Oquendo was surprised by Jason's youth, Jason was surprised at Oquendo's sociability. Oquendo was a short, stocky man with a very friendly and inviting personality. This became very evident when their conversation was interrupted several times by friends, acquaintances and even the father of one of the players, who greeted Oquendo as they passed. Everyone seemed to like Oquendo and his magnetic energy. He was very accommodating and wanted to help Jason any way he could.

"I've got meetings with some guys from the Red's front office tonight, but I can meet after that," Oquendo said.

"Look, I don't care if it's 10:30 p.m. or 2:30 a.m., I have to get this done. I have to fly home early in the morning," Jason said.

Oquendo agreed to call Jason when his meetings concluded, and they would meet at Oquendo's hotel for however long Jason needed. Jason rejoined his friends and the three decided to make their way to Wrigley Field to watch the Chicago Cubs play the Atlanta Braves. It was the Sunday Night Baseball game on ESPN and the last game before the three day All-Star break.

Unfortunately, the Cubs game was standing room only. Even Chris's and Eddie's connections in Chicago could not get them into the sold out game. As an alternative, they walked across the street from the stadium to Bar Louie, a sports bar, to watch the game on television and have a few beers and eat before Jason's meeting with Oquendo.

*   *   *

Jason was disappointed he would not be able to watch the game live. Seeing a baseball game in person was a thrill for Jason, and it always reminded him of his childhood. Jason's family, back in Texas, attended Rangers' games, usually with seats in the left field bleachers. Jason would stand the entire game, constantly popping his fist into his baseball glove, staying vigilant, hoping to snag a foul ball.

Never wanting to miss a batting practice, Jason usually demanded that his parents take him to the game at least an hour early. The excitement of the day only intensified when he would walk through the tunnel to the bleacher seats and be met by the vivid, bright green, immaculately manicured field where his favorite players roamed, shagging fly balls or taking infield practice. Even at such a young age, the speed of the game awed him.

In the fourth grade, Jason's family moved to Ardmore, Oklahoma where teams were determined by the elementary school one attended, not by tryouts. The Charles Evans team would be his new home. Jason's usual position of shortstop was already filled by a ten-year-old baseball phenom named Kendrick Moore, so Jason moved to third base. Kendrick, whose father played minor league professional baseball, was by far the most talented player on the Charles Evans team, if not all of Ardmore. Even at ten years old, Kendrick played the position effortlessly. The talk of parents and players alike revealed that he was special. Kendrick's defensive abilities could have enabled him to play with kids three, five, or even eight years older than himself. Jason was grateful he had the opportunity to play alongside Kendrick, even if it was for only one summer. Kendrick, Jason and another team member made the All-Star team that year. Jason believed he had really made it. Their team dismantled the rest of the league, and Jason was the 'star' third baseman at the ripe old age of ten.

Over the years Jason lost touch with Kendrick, but he later ran across his former teammate when he attended law school at the University of Arkansas. At this time Kendrick was playing for the Razorback baseball team, and eventually was drafted by the Kansas City Royals, where he played in the minor leagues for several years before he retired from the game. It was no surprise Kendrick was able to play baseball professionally. Jason took pride in knowing he was once Kendrick's teammate and now, while Jason was toiling away at law school, Kendrick was using his baseball skills to make a living.

                *   *   *

Shortly before ten o'clock Oquendo called Jason to let him know his meeting had concluded. Chris drove Eddie and Jason to meet with him at his downtown hotel. Chris and Eddie would have a drink at the bar and meet with other baseball personnel while Jason interviewed Oquendo.

Jason led Oquendo to a quiet sitting area off the hotel's lobby. He turned off his cell phone and instructed Oquendo to do the same. "I need your undivided attention," Jason said. Jason believed from previous conversations with Oquendo that he had a lot of information to share regarding the grievance, and he had to make sure Oquendo was focused on the issues and was able to describe the events in even greater and more complete detail.

For the next two hours, Jason quizzed Oquendo and made careful notes of each answer. Oquendo verified each person involved along with their biographies from the beginning of the case to the very end. With each answer from Oquendo, Jason felt more comfortable with the way he would conduct discovery and document production. Oquendo's story

had not changed from their first conversation, a problem Jason
was worried about since the case was seven years old.

During this interview, Oquendo repeatedly said the
name Gordon Blakeley. Oquendo said Blakeley was with him in
Mexico to scout Michel Hernández. Blakeley was, at the time,
the Director of International Scouting for the Yankees. It was
interesting to Jason that the Yankees would send 'front office'
personnel to check out a player who had just defected, but he
filed the thought away. When the interview concluded, it was
only a few short hours before Jason's early morning flight. He
had to be home to meet his wife, Robin, for her doctor's
appointment. They were expecting in August.

Following the All-Star break and back home in
Arkansas, Jason began to organize the documents and other
evidence he needed to provide the Yankees. Jason's wife,
Robin, had been on bed rest since Jason's return from the All-
Star break which added to his mounting stress. Jason's work on
this grievance was his main focus until his wife gave birth to a
son, Colin, on July 22, 2003.

Colin was born five weeks prematurely and spent two
weeks in the Neonatal Intensive Care Unit. Jason was amazed at
how small four pounds and nine ounces could be. Seeing his
tiny child only ignited a feeling of vulnerability within himself.
He was moving into unfamiliar territory in his personal and
professional life.

During Colin's time in the Neonatal Unit, Jason
requested more time to respond to the Bill of Particulars from
Major League Baseball and the Yankees. Shortly thereafter, he

received an email from Rich Rabin, the Yankees counsel, which said Jason's request was "perfectly reasonable" and that the Yankees organization wished to pass along their "congratulations and best wishes." The tone of the email struck Jason as almost human. Perhaps there was a pulse coming from the opposing side after all.

Finally, in early August, Colin was released from the hospital, and the Brownings settled in to enjoy the new addition to their family outside of the Neonatal Intensive Care Unit, and more particularly, the incubator. Their new world, working on no sleep and amazement at how such a tiny being could dictate so much, couldn't stop Jason's thoughts that those outside his world were waiting on him. He went back to work finishing the response to the Yankees' Bill of Particulars that he had begun before Colin's arrival.

The Yankees' Bill of Particulars, dated July 21, 2003, contained fourteen questions, the answers to which they hoped would give them enough ammunition to put an end to the case. Jason spent a considerable amount of time on the phone with Alex Escalante, who served as Ricalde's interpreter, to discover and/or verify the answers. It was a slow and arduous task. Each question was posed to Alex who, in turn, relayed the translated question to Señor Ricalde. Along the way, Jason explained the significance of each question and how it pertained to the case. It was paramount for Ricalde to understand the importance of his answers and the possible repercussions, but all Jason had to rely upon was the interpreter's responses. If Jason needed faith in anything, it was in Alex, who held the balance of each answer in his interpretations.

Yankees' counsel began by asking who typed the agreement, or contract, between Yucatan and the Yankees. Counsel specifically asked for each person's full name, title and employer at the time the agreement was written.

Jason's answer was simple. Gustavo Ricalde, President of the Yucatan Lions, and Jorge Oquendo agreed to the clauses set forth in the agreement and that Jose Rivero Ancona, the General Manager of the Yucatan Lions, typed it.

The second question asked for the date, time and place, including address where the "alleged" agreement was typed. Jason felt the added "alleged" was amusing. At the very least, the frequent use of "alleged" made it clear the Yankees were going to question the validity or authenticity of the contract.

Jason responded that the agreement was typed on or about November 21, 1996, at Calle 50 #406-Entre 36Y37Col. Jesus, Carranza Merida, Yucatan, Mexico, an answer Jason had no reason to believe was anything but accurate.

The Yankees next inquired as to who reviewed the alleged agreement before it was signed. Jason knew it would have been at least Ricalde and Jorge Oquendo, but he assumed Gordon Blakeley also reviewed the contents of the document before it was signed. After all, he was the only other Yankees' personnel present.

The Yankees then asked when and where the agreement was signed by Oquendo, Ricalde and notarized by Jose Enrique Gutierrez Lopez.

Based on the information provided by Ricalde, Jason responded that all parties signed the document on November, 21 1996 at the Fiesta Americana Hotel in Merida, Yucatan, Mexico. This date was not significant at that time, or so Jason thought.

The fifth question seemed to tread over ground already covered, but this time counsel asked for the identity of, not only all persons who reviewed the agreement, but also all persons present when the alleged agreement was signed.

Yucatan's response: Ricalde, Oquendo and the notary, Gutierrez Lopez. (The occupation and title of each were once again listed).

In a slightly different twist, the next question inquired as to who negotiated the terms of the alleged agreement.

Just as he had been told by Ricalde, Jason responded by stating that Oquendo, Ricalde and Gordon Blakeley had negotiated the terms.

The following question took it one step further and asked how each of the parties mentioned in the previous question participated in the negotiations.

The response, as relayed to Jason, was a very basic recitation of the events but enough to satisfy this particular inquiry. Gustavo Ricalde presented the contract and the terms to Jorge Oquendo to review. It was believed Jorge Oquendo then took the contract to Gordon Blakeley's room at the Fiesta Americana Hotel to discuss the facts and the terms of the agreement. Gordon Blakeley informed Jorge Oquendo that the terms of the agreement were acceptable and gave Jorge

Oquendo authority to sign the agreement on behalf of the New York Yankees.

Jason was then asked to identify all employees of the Yankees who were aware the agreement was being negotiated.

He responded by saying it was understood that Gordon Blakeley called Mark Newman to discuss the terms of the agreement and to explain that the agreement was being signed by Jorge Oquendo on behalf of the Yankees.

The Yankees then wished to learn all bases for the assertion that Jorge Oquendo was the Director of Scouting for Latin America for the New York Yankees and the dates in which he held that position. In other words, they were questioning the fact that Oquendo, their own employee, worked for them in that capacity.

There were several items which could verify Oquendo's position at that time, but Jason responded that Jorge Oquendo was given the title of "Director of Scouting for Latin America" by the New York Yankees, and in particular, Gordon Blakeley. Jorge Oquendo served as the Director of Scouting for Latin America for the New York Yankees from 1992 to 1998. Carlos Paz, a scout at the time with the New York Yankees for Mexico, informed Gustavo Ricalde that Jorge Oquendo held such position.

The tenth question switched gears and delved into the substance of the contract by asking what obligations each side would have under the agreement.

Jason laid out the obligations by stating Yucatan was responsible for getting Michel Hernández to Mexico for the purposes of making him available to sign with the New York Yankees. The New York Yankees, because they were given the opportunity to sign Michel Hernández, had an obligation to pay Yucatan the agreed-upon fee in the event Michel Hernández was placed on the Yankees forty-man roster. Dissecting the obligation question even further, the Yankees asked what the Yucatan Lions had done to fulfill their obligation under the agreement.

Jason wrote that Yucatan notified Jorge Oquendo and Gordon Blakeley of Michel Hernández' availability and presence in Mexico and assured the Yankees they would have the opportunity to sign and have the rights to Michel Hernández. No other teams would be notified.

Question twelve asked Jason to state all bases on which Jorge Oquendo was alleged to have had authority to negotiate and execute the alleged agreement on behalf of the Yankees. Not only were they questioning Oquendo's position, but also implying that Oquendo had no right to negotiate the contract on their behalf.

Jason's response was similar to the one just three questions earlier: Jorge Oquendo was the Director of Scouting for Latin America for the New York Yankees and was given such title and authority by Gordon Blakeley. Gordon Blakeley gave Jorge Oquendo the authority to sign the subject agreement for the purpose of obtaining the rights to Michel Hernández.

Next, Jason was asked to identify all employees and agents of the Yankees who were aware the alleged agreement had been "executed," including the date, time, and place each such person became aware of its execution.

Again, according to Jason's information, Gordon Blakeley was aware the agreement had been executed on November 21, 1996. Blakeley had given Jorge Oquendo the authority to sign the agreement while they were both staying in the Fiesta Americana Hotel, Merida, Yucatan, Mexico. Mark Newman was aware on or about November 21, 1996. It was believed Gordon Blakeley contacted Newman by telephone in regard to the terms of the agreement.

Finally, Jason was asked for proof that the Yankees approved the agreement or proof that any employee of the Yankees ratified or approved it.

In Jason's response, he said it was understood Gordon Blakeley ratified or approved the agreement on the date the agreement was signed after Jorge Oquendo presented the agreement and discussed the terms with him. Gordon Blakeley instructed Oquendo to sign the agreement and to conclude the dealings with Yucatan for the purpose of assuring the New York Yankees' ability to obtain the rights to sign Michel Hernández to a Uniform Players Contract.

Gordon Blakeley was in Mexico to scout the talents of Michel Hernández, but he did not directly participate in the contract negotiations. That was left to Jorge Oquendo. Blakeley did not sign the contract, Oquendo did, even though Blakeley was at the same hotel at the same time the negotiations were taking place. Why did Blakeley not sign the contract if the Yankees wanted this young Cuban so desperately? Jason worried it was because the Yankees created an escape if something went wrong: they could claim Oquendo did not have the authority to sign the contract.

The Yankees' presence in Mexico alone violated MLB rules regarding unblocked players and was potentially a violation of regulations decreed by the U.S. Office of Foreign Assets Control (OFAC) regarding dealings with Cuban nationals.

OFAC is the successor to the Office of Foreign Funds Control (the "FFC"), which was created at the beginning of World War II. The FFC's initial function was to prevent Nazi use of the occupied countries' assets. The modern day OFAC was established by President Harry Truman in 1950, following China's entry into the Korean War to block all North Korean and Chinese assets subject to U.S. jurisdiction. The agency was originally named the Division of Foreign Assets Control, but the name was changed by the Department of Treasury in 1962.

The Office of Foreign Assets Control is a part of the United States Department of Treasury which dispenses and enforces trade and economic sanctions based on national security goals and U.S. foreign policy against targeted foreign states, organizations, and individuals. The sanctions are imposed against hostile countries, terrorists or terrorist-driven organizations, drug traffickers, and individuals or groups involved in the production or use of weapons of mass destruction.

Specific to Cuba is the Cuban Embargo. It is a commercial, economic, and financial embargo that was partially imposed on Cuba in October 1960. It was enacted after Cuba confiscated the properties of United States citizens and corporations in Cuba. It was strengthened to a near-total embargo on February 7, 1962. Titled the Cuban Democracy Act, the embargo was put into law in 1992 to preserve sanctions on Cuba and the Castro regime. Congress passed the Helms-Burton Act in 1996, which further limited United States citizens from conducting business in or with Cuba. In 1999, President Bill Clinton extended the trade embargo even further by terminating the practice of foreign subsidiaries of U.S. companies doing business with Cuba.

Before Oquendo signed the contract for Hernández in Mexico, he stated that he needed to have someone "look it over." That could have been no one other than Gordon Blakeley because no other Yankees' representatives were present at that time in Mexico. It looked as if the Yankees wanted the best of both sides, having Blakeley in Mexico to oversee the negotiations from afar but not having him present at the signing of the contract itself.

One of the topics Jason discussed with Oquendo while they were in Chicago was his job title and duties while with the Yankees. Jason anticipated that the Yankees were going to make an issue out of Oquendo's status as a Yankee scout and that his role with the club was minimal at best. To contest any claim that Oquendo was a mere underling in the organization, Oquendo provided Jason with a signed letter from Gordon Blakeley dated August 7, 1996 that read: *"I wanted to thank you for your significant involvement in the signing of the two Nicaraguan pitchers. You responded quickly and professionally throughout the scouting and signing process. As you are finding out, so many of the International signings are successful by using the team approach and you were a major part of that team."*

In 1996, Gordon Blakeley was so impressed by the man that he felt the need to personally thank him for his efforts and went so far as to call Oquendo "a major part of the team."

CHAPTER 4

"Players have been bought, sold and exchanged as though they were sheep instead of American citizens."
- John Montgomery Ward

In October 2003, three months after the Yankees issued the Bill of Particulars, Jason received a puzzling Fed Ex envelope from Jorge Oquendo. Inside were documents Jason had never seen. The documents were forwarded with no explanation for why they were sent to him, why Oquendo had them, or who provided them to Oquendo. This prompted another call to Oquendo. Jason pressed the scout for information surrounding his possession of these documents, but Oquendo steadfastly refused to reveal who it was that delivered them to him.

The documents totaled only four pages, but the substance was nothing short of explosive. The documents, one hand-written page and a three-page typed memorandum, were believed to be from Gordon Blakeley and Gus Dominguez. The type-written document was believed to be an unsigned interoffice memorandum from Blakeley to Mark Newman, Assistant Director of Player Development and Scouting for the Yankees. The memo was dated May 30, 1999 and was an admonishment of two Yankees' accountants who had questioned several items on Blakeley's travel expense reports.

The letter began innocently enough, but it contained incredible details of trips and expenses. Blakeley defended the expenses in question by listing the players he had scouted, complete with dates and locations. He even explained that his airfare for a May trip was $250 cheaper by choosing a flight with a stop in Denver rather than opting for a direct flight to Chicago. The substance of the memo was specific in detail. One interesting item listed was $32.87 spent on cigars given to

Gus Dominguez, the very agent involved in getting Michel Hernández out of Mexico for Blakeley and the Yankees.

Page two of the memo expounded on the money Blakeley spent out of his own pocket that he never submitted for reimbursement. Some items, in particular, were incredible: *"Mark, as you are well aware of, I have been a travel warrior extending myself in all aspects of my job. I have put my personal life a distant second and this job you have trusted to me at the highest level possible. I have spent hundreds of dollars out of my own pockets to bribe agents, parents and players. I have never claimed any of these and have given Cuban players over $1,000 during the past 3 years as a New York Yankee. I lost several hundred dollars in Japan on each trip trying to secure Hideki Irabu. I find it insulting that I am questioned about meals, tickets and entertainment by the accounting department, Dan Matheson and Rigo Garcia whom sleep in their own bed every night. I have worked very hard to have a large part in securing New York Yankees prospects as well as giving information to the group in putting together the major league team."* The letter closes with a veiled threat: *"I have been a loyal employee for the New York Yankees and for me not to be trusted probably means I should go to another organization."* The tone of the memo revealed Blakeley had grown tired of his seemingly thankless and costly efforts for the betterment of the Yankees' organization.

Two years prior to the date this letter was written, the Yankees signed Hideki Irabu, who was mentioned in the Blakeley letter, to a four-year, $13 million dollar contract. Many believed George Steinbrenner was on a personal mission to sign the hard-throwing Japanese pitcher. Immediately officials from the Japanese League called for an investigation, alleging the Yankees tampered with negotiations for Irabu by contacting the pitcher before the Yankees had the rights to do so. This, they said, was a direct violation of a 1967 treaty which regulated interaction between Japanese baseball organizations and Major League Baseball. The San Diego Padres, through a working agreement with Irabu's Japanese team, originally held the negotiating rights to the pitcher, but Irabu said he did not want to sign with any team other than the Yankees, so a deal was made. Eventually the controversy faded and Irabu went on to pitch three seasons with the Yankees.

The second, hand-written letter Jason received from Oquendo was one page, unsigned, and rather cryptic. It was believed to have been written by Gus Dominguez, with comments scribbled in the margins, presumably by Gordon Blakeley. It contained a short list of players and their respective contract terms, including length of time and salary. Directly below this list is a line that reads: *"$11,250,000 – Total (4 players)"* The next line reads: *"$2,000,000 – to G.D. cash to pre-agree."* With an arrow pointing to the two million dollar figure, the next line said: *"$500,000 to G.B. to get it done from G.D."*

Jason assumed the G.D. to be Gus Dominguez, and, likewise, the G.B. he assumed to be Gordon Blakeley. Apparently $11.25 million was to secure the four players, and two million of that was to go to Gus Dominguez. Then

Dominguez would pay Blakeley a half a million dollars out of his cut to "get the deal done."

The next statement on the letter related directly to Michel Hernandez. It read: *"On Michel H'dez – Please take all payments made to me off the books. I was sent a 1099 and this should be taken off. Cubas cannot have anything on us. Also, Michel cannot be told that we were paid expenses by the Yankees either."*

Gus Dominguez must not have wanted his name to be connected with Michel Hernández. At a certain point, Michel fired Gus Dominguez as his agent and signed with Joe Cubas, which would give Dominguez a very good reason to be so concerned. In another interesting twist, Dominguez seemed to be charging Hernández for business expenses that were already being reimbursed by the Yankees.

Jason understood the significance of these statements, yet he found it remarkable that anyone would detail such "kickbacks" in writing. It was almost too manufactured, he thought. Surely Oquendo would not concoct something like this. Why would this documentation not have been destroyed when the risk of it being discovered, and used, was so great? Jason examined the memo and believed that it was authentic, but he could hardly believe that he was holding it.

The story of one particular player listed on the document, Andy Morales, helped reveal not only when the document was written, but also that it really could have been written by sports agent Gus Dominguez. In 1999 a historical

BRAYAN PEÑA - C - 17 (3 YRS. - $5 MIL. PACKAGE) Mid May. to Costa Rica

ZEROY OUT OF WBA IND WITH ME

MIGUEL PEREZ - RHP - 25 (3 YRS. - $2.5 MIL. PACKAGE)

JULIO CESAR VILLELON - RHP - 22 (3 YRS. - $1.75 MIL. PACKAGE)

NATANIEL REINOSO - OF - 26

ALEXIS HERNANDEZ - C - 26 } UP TO YOU   to Costa Rica

JUAN CARLOS BRUZON - OF - 27

WILL GET IN BALT. THIS WKND.

ANDY MORALES - 3B - 25   (3 YRS. - $2.0 MIL. PACKAGE)

$11,250,000 - TOTAL (4 PLAYERS)

$2,040,000 - TO G.D. CASH TO PRE-AGREE

($500,000 TO G.B TO GET IT DONE.
FROM G.D.

• ON Michel H'DEZ — PLEASE TAKE ALL PAYMENTS MADE
TO ME OFF-THE BOOKS. I WAS SENT
A 1099 AND THIS SHOULD BE TAKEN
OFF. CUBANS CANNOT HAVE ANYTHING
ON US. ALSO, MICHEL CANNOT BE
TOLD THAT WE WERE PAID EXPENSES
BY THE YANKEES EITHER.

• WHAT DO YOU THINK OF MICHAEL JOVA (IN COSTA RICA?)

pair of exhibition games was played. The Baltimore Orioles
traveled to Cuba to play the Cuban National Team on March
28th and then, in May, the Cuban team came to Baltimore to
play the Orioles at Camden Yards. One of the stars of the Cuban
team was third baseman Andy Morales. On the mysterious
hand-written document, Andy Morales' name was singled out
and next to his name was written *'will get in Balt. this wknd'.*
Also written was the number '25' which Jason assumed to be
Morales' age at that time. Finally, next to his age was written *'3
years - $2 mil. package.'* Gus Dominguez must have had plans
to meet Morales that weekend in Baltimore, and he already had
thoughts of his market value. Further, he was presumably
sharing his thoughts and intentions with Blakeley.

    According to a February 14, 2001 article in the New
York Times, Cuban authorities witnessed Morales talking with
Dominguez while in Baltimore and quickly removed Morales
from the Cuban National Team upon his return to Cuba.
Apparently, the discussions between Morales and Dominguez
prompted Cuban authorities to believe Morales would defect, so
Morales was deemed to be a flight risk. Although the Cuban
government kept a close eye on him, he returned to Cuba
following the game to a hero's welcome, with fans cheering his
three-run homer in his team's victory against the Orioles.

    From that point forward, life was unpleasant for Morales
in his home country. According to another New York Times
article dated July 20, 2000, a spokesman for Gus Dominguez,
Rene Guim, was quoted as saying, "Cuban security people were
following him everywhere." A week prior to his interview,

Guim said Morales had gotten into "a little push and shove" encounter with three of these security guards. Guim said, "They pushed him in an alley and beat the heck out of him. I think that's probably what broke the camel's back."

Morales wanted to get out of Cuba, not only for the sake of his baseball career, but now because he feared for his life. In June of 2000, Morales, along with several other Cubans, attempted to flee to the United States in a speedboat hired to smuggle the illegal cargo. Unfortunately, the boat ran out of gas just twenty-five miles off of the Florida coast. The crew and passengers were detained by the U.S. Coast Guard. Morales sought political asylum but failed to convince authorities he would be in imminent danger if he returned to Cuba.

In an unprecedented move, President Clinton's administration became deeply involved in the matter and decided to send the passengers of that dangerous trip back to Cuba. It was a hard-line enforcement of the "wet foot, dry foot" policy, which stated that a Cuban who made it to United States soil could apply for residency in one year, but for defectors captured at sea, a return trip to Cuba was required. A June 8, 2000 New York Times article stated, "The administration's position appeared to signal a hardening toward Cubans who defy established procedures for immigrating to the United States." Though Morales was unable to convince American authorities of the dangers awaiting him upon his return to Cuba, Florida Congresswoman Ileana Ros-Lehtinen was quoted in the same article as saying, "It's going to be very hard for him. His life will be in jeopardy."

Morales would not be deterred. On July 19, 2000, Morales, along with eight others, succeeded in reaching the United States. Shortly after his arrival Morales met up again with his agent, Gus Dominguez, who told him that he had to establish residency in another country before he could become a free agent. Peru was the preferred choice, but the paperwork sent to Major League Baseball by the Peruvian government said Morales had not been granted residency, but had erroneously received "refugee" status.

After re-submitting the paperwork, Morales received his Peruvian residency and was declared a free agent. Teams interested in Morales had the opportunity to make offers and from such, Morales was free to choose his employer. Supposedly, the Yankees outbid three teams; Morales became a Yankee. He ultimately signed a four-year deal worth $4.5 million, two years after his meeting with Gus Dominguez in Baltimore, and presumably, two years after the memo detailing Gus Dominguez's intentions.

Immediately, concerns and doubts began to arise over his age. At that time Morales was listed as 26 but some within the baseball community believed he was several years older. Nevertheless, Morales began to work out for the Yankees. After reporting to spring training in 2001, the level of Morales' skills were also questioned. Anticipated to be the successor to the Yankees' third baseman Scott Brosius, Morales struggled at the plate and was optioned to the Yankees' AA affiliate, the Norwich Navigators.

His success at the AA level was minimal and the Yankees sought to have Morales' contract voided. The Yankees cited evidence that allegedly contradicted his stated age of twenty-six. Morales claimed he was born in 1974, but the Yankees claimed they obtained information that proved he was born in 1971.

Questions about the age of Cuban players were nothing new. In March 1998, Orlando Hernández signed a $6.6 million deal with the Yankees and became known for his postseason dominance. He was reportedly born in 1971, but documents related to a court case showed he was actually born in 1965. Rey Ordonez, another Cuban defector, signed a four-year contract with the New York Mets worth $19 million in 2000. Major League Baseball listed 1972 as his year of birth but Ordonez himself, in 1997, said he was born in 1971. Although a grievance was filed by the Major League Baseball Players Association on behalf of Andy Morales, he never played a single game in the major leagues.

Jason was stunned by the mysterious documents provided by Oquendo. Only a small portion of the text was arguably related to the Lions' case, but he knew he must find a way to introduce the letters into the grievance proceedings. If nothing else, the letters could shed some light on Gordon Blakeley's practices for the Commissioner's office. At the same time, Jason had strong, legitimate questions about these mysterious documents. Where did they come from? Why were they delivered to Oquendo? Why would they have been kept for so many years? Yet, Oquendo never revealed his source. To this day, it remains unknown who sent these documents to the scout. Did this mysterious person have knowledge that Jason's case was pending?

As much as the substance of these documents was controversial, there were many more questions surrounding their authenticity. However, details from each made it virtually impossible for anybody but Blakeley and Dominguez to have written. Jason knew their validity would be questioned, but with the details of the information contained in the documents, like the one involving Andy Morales, Jason hoped the documents could be proven authentic.

In November 2003, after the Yankees received Jason's response to their Bill of Particulars, they submitted a Pre-Trial Motion in Support of Dismissal to the Commissioner's office. Apparently, they felt there was little to support the claims of the Yucatan Lions so the case should be dropped. They also pointed out several inconsistencies in the story. One of these inconsistencies would dog Jason throughout the remainder of the grievance process.

In the Bill of Particulars, the Yankees requested information surrounding the contract, including times, places and people involved. One such request was for the date the contact was signed. Immediately, the Yankees honed in on Jason's answer: November 21, 1996. The Yankees relentlessly hammered on the point saying, "This proves the contact is fraudulent. Gordon Blakeley was in Japan on the date the agreement was supposedly signed." This was the first Jason had heard of the misdating. Blakeley was in Japan? Jason was dumbfounded. He was concerned this would be the death of the case. It was difficult to contradict the evidence supplied by the Yankees. Blakeley's passport, hotel and airline receipts showed he was not in Mexico at the time in question.

Frustrated, and feeling he had been misled, Jason called Señor Ricalde, hoping for a good explanation. Through Ricalde's translator, Jason quizzed his client. Adding to the difficulty in prosecuting the grievance was the obstacle of working through a translator.

Jason explained that he had received a copy of the motion for dismissal, which stated that the contract could not be genuine because Gordon Blakeley was in Japan at the time it was signed. Ricalde confirmed that the contract was signed three weeks earlier, he believed on, or about, the third of November. Jason was stunned. He wanted to know why he had not been told this earlier. Ricalde told Jason that he was not completely certain of the reason why the contract was purposefully misdated, but he did remember it was the Yankees who requested the change in dates. Jason pressed for more information; he wanted to know why this happened and why he wasn't told. Ricalde could not answer the question of why, but he had always assumed the contract was misdated so the Yankees could deny its authenticity if any trouble ever arose.

Such a response only convoluted the factual history giving rise to the agreement, and Ricalde's explanation caused Jason even greater concern about the viability of the grievance. Not only was Jason concerned with his client's posture in the proceedings, but he was astonished that such events could or would transpire. It was perplexing to say the least.

Jason asked Ricalde if he knew who ordered the contract to be misdated. Ricalde could not say for certain, but the only two Yankees' representatives in Mexico on the date the contract was written and signed were Jorge Oquendo and Gordon Blakeley. Jason now needed proof of Oquendo and Blakeley's presence in Mexico on the correct date, November third, and he asked if Ricalde could help get this information. Ricalde said he knew the manager of the hotel where the two men stayed during their visit. He was certain he could obtain the proof Jason needed.

Within the week, Jason received hotel receipts from Ricalde. What Jason had felt to be a fatal blow to his client's case was diffused by confirmation that Oquendo and Blakeley were indeed in Merida, Mexico, on November 3rd. Now the issue was firming up why the contract was postdated. Setting aside the Yankees' assertions of fraud, the questions lingered as to whether the Yankees ever intended to abide by the terms. If the Yankees were so concerned with making their presence unknown while in Mexico, why even sign such an agreement? The most logical reason would be that Ricalde would not let Michel leave Mexico if he didn't have such an agreement in place. Jason was concerned now with having to prove the authenticity of the agreement by such a delicate rationale.

Jason learned from Ricalde that a private workout was held for Hernández at the Yucatan Lions stadium where Gordon Blakeley, Jorge Oquendo and Carlos Paz from the Yankees first got to see the talents of the young player. The Yankees' representatives witnessed Hernández hit, catch, throw and run. No others were allowed in the stadium during the workout and no other players participated. Hernández had a little power at the plate but was mainly a defensive player. He was, in scouting terms, a 'catch and throw' player. Details of the workout were scant due to the small number of those present and the fact that the Yankees specifically requested no one be told of the day's activities, including the Mexican media. Apparently, the Yankees were impressed enough to continue negotiations for Hernández after the workout and after returning to the hotel.

*   *   *

Jason often wondered how a scouting report would read on him. "Slow, can't hit, but can catch the ball." The defensive aspect of baseball always interested Jason the most. While other kids his age practiced their hitting, Jason fielded hundreds of ground balls hit to him by his father. After he came home from work, Jason's father would take Jason across the street to a junior high school ball field. For two and half hours every day he would do nothing but field ground balls. He believed his slight stature was the main reason why hitting was not a priority; he would leave hitting to the bigger guys. This is where he learned the art of fielding; it just came naturally to him. Never stand on the heels, always on the balls of the feet. Keep the glove on the ground, work "ground up." Have soft hands… lessons that served him for years to come.

Following his years in the Babe Ruth league, Jason played American Legion ball as well as for his high school, the

Southside Rebels in Fort Smith. Defensively, Jason was a polished, well-rounded player, but around this time he realized his lack of proficiency at the plate was starting to become a liability. His junior year was Southside's first year to have a baseball team, yet they made it all the way to the state tournament. However, Jason didn't see much action due to his inability to hit. During his senior year of high school in 1991, Jason visited Hendrix College in Conway, Arkansas. Since his mother was a teacher, getting a good education was paramount in his family. The opportunity to apply to Hendrix, a well-respected private, liberal arts college, was one his mom would not let pass.

Just as in high school, Hendrix was forming a baseball program and was in the midst of moving from the Arkansas Intercollegiate Conference (AIC) to the Southern Collegiate Athletic Conference (SCAC), a division three conference in the NCAA. The conference was comprised of several academically-oriented schools such as Rhodes College in Memphis, Tennessee, Millsaps in Jackson, Mississippi, and Trinity in San Antonio, Texas. The baseball coach at Hendrix was from Van Buren, Arkansas, just across the Arkansas River from Fort Smith, and he knew Jason's high school baseball coach. Jason was invited to play for Hendrix. The new conference was a non-scholarship conference, but an education from a school like Hendrix was worth it.

During Jason's sophomore year, the conference move was complete, and Hendrix finally had their new baseball team. The team began preparing for the season, as all colleges do, in the cold of January, which was no friend to an athlete. During a practice Jason suffered an impingement of his right shoulder while fielding a ground ball and throwing it to first base. An orthopedic surgeon in Fort Smith told Jason that he had very little of the bursa sac still intact, which was causing a severe case of bursitis. The bursa sac served as a lubricant for the ball and socket joint of the shoulder. Without it, the shoulder joint was essentially working bone against bone.

The doctor gave Jason two options: he could have surgery to repair the shoulder and miss his entire sophomore season or take Cortisone shots which would allow him to continue to play baseball. Jason opted for the shots, which were administered by a doctor with a large needle around the shoulder joint, injecting the medication in multiple locations. The needle would be inserted and repositioned, and the Cortisone burned like hell. On a cold, icy day in January 2003, Jason left the doctor's office consumed with pain and slipped into his car before realizing a new dilemma, his car was a standard. He could barely move his shoulder but driving would require both arms. Needless to say, it was an excruciating drive home.

Jason knew, unfortunately, that his baseball career would be over following Hendrix. He wanted to be able to build a professional career somewhat close to his beloved game, but how to accomplish that was still a big unknown. Jason visited with the college counselor during his senior year, to ask how he could find a career within the world of sports. Fortunately, the

counselor had just received information on an upcoming sports
law conference in New York.

Jason discussed the idea with his parents, and in January
of 1995 Jason flew to New York to attend his first sports law
symposium. The keynote speaker was none other than David
Faulk, a well-known attorney and Michael Jordan's agent.
During one of the breaks at the symposium, Jason approached
Mr. Faulk to discuss his interest and find out how he could keep
baseball in his life. Mr. Faulk's immediate and unwavering
advice was, "Go to law school."

Jason was in awe. If Mr. Faulk would have told him to
go shine shoes, Jason would have run out and purchased a
polishing cloth. Based on his advice, Jason made the decision to
apply to the law school at the University of Arkansas.

This was Jason's first trip to New York, and he took
advantage of some down time to tour the more notorious
attractions. Wandering the streets and feeling engulfed by all
the buildings, Jason had no idea that in the years to come, New
York would serve as the backdrop for his legal entanglement
with the historic New York Yankees.

CHAPTER 5

"One of the beautiful things about baseball is that every once in a while you come into a situation where you want to, and where you have to, reach down and prove something."
-Nolan Ryan

On November 3, 2003, Jason sent a letter to Rich Rabin informing him of the mysterious documents he had received from Oquendo. Jason knew the documents could be explosive and controversial, so he asked for a private phone call to discuss the document's contents.

In his letter, Jason stated, *"I am in possession of two documents pertaining to Gordon Blakeley or purported to have been drafted by Mr. Blakeley while employed with the New York Yankees. Although there has been no specific confidentiality agreement agreed to between our respective clients, I submit that we discuss the nature of these documents in confidence before I submit them as an exhibit at Mr. Blakeley's deposition. Please contact me to discuss."*

In his letter of response dated two days later, Rabin dismissed Jason's suggestion and expressed there was no need to discuss the documents. He said, *"I have received your correspondence of November 3, 2003. As you know, the Yankees have filed a motion to dismiss this matter, and we are confident that this litigation will not and cannot proceed. The depositions you reference thus will not proceed, and the discovery issues you raise are moot."* This last sentence echoed in Jason's mind. He knew he was in possession of some significant information, and for it to be deemed "moot" might prove to be a misstep by the Yankees. Their confidence that the case would be dismissed would be a common theme throughout this case. They were adamant that the case held no merit.

In a letter of response, though, to the Yankees' motion for dismissal dated March 22, 2004, Allan "Bud" Selig,

Commissioner of Baseball, stated: *"The Professional Baseball Agreement provides that the Commissioner decides this dispute as arbitrator ... After careful consideration of all the information submitted by the parties to this dispute, I deny the Yankees' motion and order that the discovery phase of the grievance should proceed. The Yankees have not demonstrated that there are no circumstances that would make the agreement enforceable. On its face, the alleged Lions-Yankees agreement is not a prohibited agreement between the Yankees and Hernández. Rather, it is an agreement between the Lions and the Yankees, the purposes and operation of which have not been established at this stage in the grievance. The Yankees are free to argue at a later time that the contract should not be enforced, but they may do so only upon a factual record. The parties should re-commence discovery according to any schedule that my staff may set on my behalf, as arbitrator."*

Clearly, the Commissioner of Major League Baseball felt there was enough evidence to proceed or, at least, a lack of irrefutable proof from the Yankees that the matter should be dropped entirely. Jason was pleased with the ruling. It appeared that MLB was taking this seriously and was going to give it the requisite time and attention. Jason wanted to ensure that the facts of the case were brought to light, and Commissioner Selig had given him the necessary opportunity to do just that.

Nearly a year and a half after Jason was introduced to Ricalde, Selig ordered the case to continue. Depositions of all the key witnesses were scheduled for the last week in June, 2004. The depositions would take place in Tampa, Florida. The

Yankees have an office in New York, but their home office and spring training facility are in Tampa. At the time that the Tampa office was established, the media - primarily the New York press - ran a number of stories about the "split offices" and how this caused a bitter power struggle within the Yankees organization. In recent years, Steinbrenner, mainly for health reasons, spent more time in Florida. Many of their executives lived and worked out of Tampa. At the time of the grievance, two of those executives included Gordon Blakeley and Mark Newman. Mark Newman joined the Yankees organization in 1989 as the Director of Player Development. Currently, Newman is the Senior Vice President, Baseball Operations for the Yankees. He works closely with General Manager, Brian Cashman on player development and scouting.

After the depositions were scheduled, Jason arranged for Señor Ricalde, Ricalde's translator and Oquendo to fly in on the Sunday before the depositions began in order to work on some final preparations. He made hotel reservations and scheduled a videographer and stenographer to record the proceedings. Jason and the Yankees' counsel would finally get to question each respective participant in the unfolding drama.

Though Jason never heard anything back from Rich Rabin regarding the mysterious documents, several days prior to the beginning of the depositions, and following discovery protocol, Jason called Michelle Burg, an associate working with Rabin on the case, to inform her of the documents and their explosive content. She asked that he fax the documents to her. Jason faxed the documents, not only to Burg, but also to the

Commissioner's office. If he planned to use the documents in any way, he had to submit them to all parties involved in the case. Otherwise, the arbitrator would potentially not allow them to be used as an exhibit.

At nearly five o'clock on the Friday afternoon before the depositions, Jason received a fax at work from the office of Yankees' counsel. The Yankees cancelled the depositions without warning or stating any reason. Jason was baffled and furious at the short notice. The depositions were to begin the following week. He rushed to contact Ricalde and Oquendo, and then he attempted to cancel the flight and hotel reservations in Tampa. He successfully reached Ricalde and Oquendo, but he could not cancel the flights. Jason immediately drafted a letter to the Commissioner's office relaying the events and insisting that the Yankees reimburse Yucatan for the costs.

The more Jason thought about the last-minute cancellation, the more Jason's perplexity grew. He thought Rich Rabin was already in Tampa going over testimony with Gordon Blakeley, so why the sudden change of plans? Suddenly the idea struck him – he had faxed over those powerful documents just days before. Maybe those documents were anything but "moot" now.

Oquendo wanted to know more of the circumstances surrounding the cancellation, so he called Lou Melendez at the Major League Baseball Commissioner's office. Melendez told Oquendo that Jason's fax of the Blakeley and Dominguez documents to the Commissioner's office "sent the entire office into an uproar." Apparently they were scrambling to find out just what this "kid from Arkansas" had.

The next day, Saturday, Jason's itinerary shifted from preparing for his flight to Tampa, to mundane yard work. However, his mind never left the case. There was little he could really do at that point, but he felt that he needed to at least talk to someone about it. He took a break from mowing his lawn and called Joe Cubas, the agent who was known to help Cuban players, and who Jason had hoped would be a witness if necessary. Jason described the events of the previous day. Cubas found the Yankees' action humorous and stated that the Yankees cancelled the depositions because they knew Jason was in a good position, and that now he had the "full attention of both the Yankees and the Commissioner's office."

Jason thought to himself that it was way too early in the game for anybody to be in the driver's seat, but things sure were getting intense fast. The grievance had officially escalated, heading in a direction that he had never anticipated. The conversation did little to subdue the feelings of urgency and aggravation within Jason, but he took comfort in how many people seemed to be in his corner. He was also feeling proud of the fact that he now had evidence that not even the Commissioner's office had.

In September, 2004 depositions were finally rescheduled. This time they would take place in New York at the office of the Commissioner of Major League Baseball. Jason arranged for Señor Ricalde, Jorge Oquendo, and Eddie Diaz to arrive on Tuesday, September 7th, a day before the depositions were to begin, in order to go over each man's testimony. The Yankees and Jason each wanted to have their own translator present during Ricalde's deposition. Eddie Diaz was Jason's choice. Eddie had a history of managing in the Mexican League and was very knowledgeable of the game. Jason didn't trust anyone other than Eddie to help with such a significant task.

Jason was the first to arrive at the Midtown Marriott on Lexington Avenue. After checking in, he retrieved the four boxes of documents he had shipped to the hotel earlier in the week. Once in his room, Jason booted up his computer and checked his emails. There was one from Rich Rabin, the Yankees' counsel, asking if the depositions would proceed as scheduled. Jason called Mr. Rabin to confirm.

"Yes, we're still on. Señor Ricalde, Mr. Oquendo and Eddie Diaz should be in shortly," Jason said as he glanced around the small, overpriced New York hotel room.

"Okay, you guys need anything, let me know," Rabin said.

"We're just a couple of blocks from the Commissioner's office; we should be fine."

"All right, I guess we'll see you in the morning."

Jason walked to the window of his room and drew back the curtain to check the view of the brick wall of an adjacent building. The hotel had been recommended by Ed Burns of the Commissioner's office due to its close proximity to the depositions. Jason closed the curtain and walked back to his computer. The view didn't matter; he was not going to have time for sightseeing. Between prepping his witnesses for the depositions and the depositions themselves, his week would be challenging. But more importantly, this case was what Jason had been waiting for, a chance to merge his passion for baseball with his practice of law. All his hard work and dedication during law school had paid off. He, a young lawyer from Arkansas, was about to come face-to-face with lawyers who were products of some of the most prestigious schools in the country, and who were representing one of the most historic franchises in sports history.

       *   *   *

    Jason studied hard in law school, except during baseball season. He vividly remembered watching Cal Ripkin break Lou Gehrig's record of consecutive games played in September of 1995, his first year of law school. After watching this, Jason reflected on his love of the game, but more importantly he stepped back to realize how unhappy he was in law school. He viewed baseball as his salvation and knew that law school was simply a means to an end. His roommate during his first year of law school, Brent Gregg, was a former teammate from Hendrix who was working towards his masters in English. Luckily, for Jason, his roommate was a die-hard St. Louis Cardinals fan and the two had a connection through baseball that helped Jason tolerate his situation. It was just like college all over again when Jason and his roommate Todd Jeffery spent many a night discussing baseball or watching a game on TV.

    Having survived law school, Jason wanted to polish his legal writing skills, so he applied for a judicial clerkship with the Arkansas Supreme Court under Justice Robert L. Brown. Although he had a law review article published in 1998, his third year in law school, Jason still wanted to concentrate on his research and writing skills. During this time Jason ran into a family friend, Jim Dunn, a senior partner at the Warner, Smith and Harris law firm in Fort Smith. Mr. Dunn scheduled an interview for Jason, one that took place before he was to meet with Justice Brown. Jason didn't know it at the time, but Warner, Smith and Harris had not hired a new attorney in quite some time, and they were looking for a bright, young attorney to join the firm.

Jason ultimately received a job offer from Warner, Smith and Harris with one caveat: the deadline for acceptance was set before his interview for the Supreme Court clerkship. Jason immediately called Justice Brown to ask if their appointment could be moved up. Such a request, Jason thought, was unthinkable coming from a third-year law student, but he did not want to miss the opportunity to meet with the esteemed Justice Brown and explore the clerkship. Justice Brown politely accommodated and the two met shortly thereafter in Little Rock. The interview was basic enough. Justice Brown quizzed Jason about his law review article and his experience in law school. Most of the conversation revolved around the Warner, Smith and Harris law firm. Justice Brown was familiar with most of the attorneys at the firm and ultimately told Jason that his time as a clerk could be better spent in private practice, getting real-world experience. Justice Brown recommended Jason take the job at the Warner firm, which had an impeccable reputation. Jason would be foolish not to capitalize on such an opportunity.

Before he began his career at Warner, Smith and Harris, Jason made it clear that he would like to pursue work in baseball. He wanted to make certain this would not be an issue and the partners agreed. A partner, Pat Moore, was already a huge baseball fan, and Jason's interview with him mainly consisted of baseball talk. Ultimately, everyone agreed to let Jason pursue the baseball avenue as long as he maintained his litigation practice.

Within his first year of practice, Jason sent his résumé out to a list of sports agents specializing in baseball. Before long Jason received a call from Chris Fanta, an agent and a partner in Pro-Talent, Inc., a sports agency based in Chicago. The two hit it off immediately. They were the same age and both had played baseball at small colleges. Chris needed an attorney because his business was beginning to flourish, and everything he read and learned about Jason fit perfectly for his operation.

Before Jason could represent any player on a given team's forty-man roster, he had to become certified by the Major League Baseball Players Association. This was a rather formalized process. The first step was to have a player-agent designation form signed by a major league player designating Jason as his agent. At that time, one of Chris Fanta's clients was Angel "Sandy" Martinez. Sandy was with the Chicago Cubs and was the catcher for Kerry Woods during his historic twenty strikeout game in 1998. Chris Fanta's agency, Pro-Talent, Inc.

added Jason to its certification, and Sandy signed off on it. Jason then filled out and submitted the application to the Players Association, which basically notified them that he would now be serving as counsel for the Pro-Talent agency. The Players Association accepted and approved Jason's application and he became certified.

The Players Association is very selective in approving agents. If they find anything out of the ordinary on an application, it will be denied. Jason's first application garnered a call from Michael Wiener, General Counsel for the Players Association. Weiner commented that he thought it was great that Pro-Talent was looking to add an attorney to their operation. He asked Jason to make one small correction to his application and resubmit. This began Jason's journey into the business side of baseball.

Each March, he traveled to spring training to help Chris with a variety of issues, and each December he attended Major League Baseball's Winter Meetings. Jason felt 2002 and 2003 were some of the most exciting times of his life. He may not have been playing baseball, but he was beginning to become immersed in the transactional side of the game.

Although Jason understood his contributions to the game were minute, he took great satisfaction in working with Chris on his numerous issues, no matter how large or small. It was those contributions that made suffering through law school worth it.

*   *   *

On the Tuesday evening before the depositions were set to begin and once all parties arrived, Jason, Señor Ricalde, and Eddie Diaz met in Ricalde's room to begin the preparation. Ricalde was scheduled to be deposed first on Wednesday, so Jason started on his testimony. Ricalde was relaxed during the prep but Jason wondered how he would react under questioning the following day.

"Okay look, just simply tell the truth. You have nothing to hide," Jason said as he began to go over the general instructions given to witnesses before depositions. "Only answer the questions asked. Don't elaborate; be short with your answers."

This statement seemed to get Ricalde's attention, and Jason could now see concern on his client's face. Señor Ricalde was new to this process, and not knowing how the process would play out was cause for concern. Jason's preparation consisted of not only shoring up the events as they occurred but instilling a sense of calmness in Ricalde so that he could testify with as little angst or trepidation possible.

Jason tried to reassure Ricalde, "Listen, don't be concerned. There's going to be a lot of shit brought up by the Yankees, but don't worry; the Commissioner's office already knows most of what has happened. They gave us permission to proceed with this, so you are not in the wrong. I simply want you to recap the timeline of events. Now let's go over it from the beginning."

It was obvious that Ricalde was uncomfortable with what was about to happen, but he also knew it had to be done.

He felt he had been wronged, and if going through this lengthy legal process made it right, he would comply. These proceedings contradicted Ricalde's personality. Jason felt Ricalde never gave much thought to the Yankees' actions while they were in Mexico and, ultimately, everything would be fine. But Ricalde never imagined the Yankees would go back on their word; this was unthinkable in his mind. Where he came from, honesty was an assumed trait. He was accustomed to taking things at face value. It had to be difficult for Ricalde to understand how the Yankees could ignore an agreement.

Shortly before midnight, Jason was satisfied Ricalde was ready. Ricalde and Diaz went to bed, but Jason could not sleep. Within hours, he would have a chance to do what most sports attorneys only dream of – going up against the New York Yankees. This was beyond negotiating a multi-year contract for a player; this was a legitimate dispute that involved convoluted facts and intrigue. This certainly was unlike any litigation Jason had handled in his practice.

The following morning, Jason, Ricalde and Diaz had breakfast in the hotel restaurant. The conversation was light and did not concern the depositions. Everyone appeared to be relaxed, but Jason knew they were all just as anxious as he was. After breakfast, the three stepped outside the hotel into a rain storm. The Commissioner's office was only a few blocks away, but it was raining so hard that walking was out of the question. Jason hailed a taxi and the group climbed into the car. Within five minutes the taxi delivered the group to 245 Park Avenue. Upon arrival, each of them had to pass through a metal detector and have their photos taken for their respective security badges. Each signed in and the guard phoned the Commissioner's office to verify the visitors' appointment.

Once cleared, they took the elevator to the thirty-first floor. The elevator doors opened to gold-faced lettering that read Major League Baseball and covered nearly the entire wall. The finish was polished to a mirror shine. When Jason saw the logo, the reality of the situation struck him, and he pulled Eddie Diaz aside. Jason knew Eddie had not experienced anything like this, and he wanted to make certain Eddie was in the right state of mind.

"Eddie," Jason whispered, "This is serious. No bullshit today, all right? Just stay focused and on task." This was an attempt to soothe his own nerves more than an admonishment of Eddie.

Eddie looked at Jason puzzled, "Sure man."

Jason and his group walked over to the front desk where they were met by two female receptionists. "We're here to see Ed Burns," Jason said to one of the receptionists, who appeared annoyed by the interruption.

"And you are?"

"Jason Browning."

"I'll let him know you are here. You can wait in the lobby," she said, while pointing back over Jason's shoulder toward the reception area.

The group entered the lobby where Jason was awestruck again by the décor. On the walls hung poster-sized aerial photographs of each Major League Baseball team's stadium, each held within its own respective shadow box. Ricalde and Diaz sat down but Jason wandered about, taking in the history contained within the room. Along with the stadium photos were bats, batting helmets and baseballs embossed with each team's logo.

Jason was engrossed in the memorabilia when the elevator chimed and the doors opened to unload the Yankees' contingent. Jason turned to watch the group enter the lobby. Each member of the Yankees' legal team was wrapped in a dark overcoat which gave the group a menacing look. In the lead was Rich Rabin, Yankees' counsel. Next to Mr. Rabin was Michelle Burg, an associate with Mr. Rabin's law firm, followed by Lonn Trost, the very man who threatened to bring Ricalde's accusations to the attention of the FBI at the onset of the case. Trost was followed by Jean Afterman, Assistant General Manager of the Yankees. Jason recognized them all. He recognized Rabin from the bio on his law firm's website and the Yankees' representatives from articles in various sports media he had read as a baseball fan throughout the years.

Jean Afterman was hired by the Yankees in December 2001. She had previously worked for sports agent Don Nomura and represented Japanese players banned from playing in Major League Baseball by an agreement between the Japanese and American professional baseball leagues in 1967. Afterman specialized in finding ways around this agreement and ultimately helped many Japanese players to MLB contracts, most notably Hideki Irabu and Hideo Nomo. When asked about the situation surrounding the forty year-old agreement,

Afterman was quoted as saying, "It wasn't just baseball; it was human rights and baseball." In 2003, Ms. Afterman was instrumental in signing Hideki Matsui for the Yankees. Yankees' General Manager, Brian Cashman has said of Afterman, "She is tough as they come and one of the smartest people I know." Afterman is considered to be on the short list of those considered to be the best candidate for the first female General Manager in Major League Baseball.

Jason's group met their adversaries in front of the reception desk. The Yankees' representatives focused their attention on Señor Ricalde. The attorneys must have been curious to meet the man who had caused so much turbulence. The groups were exchanging pleasantries when Ed Burns arrived to greet the parties and escort everyone to the conference room. The room was a spacious, corner conference area. Two walls were solid glass which gave the room's guests an unfettered view of a sea of skyscrapers. Jason strode over to the windows to survey the city. Buildings and skyscrapers were lined up like dominoes against the dark grey sky of the stormy day. The cars formed lines of traffic that snaked through the city's streets. Pedestrians were like ants marching in a disorderly fashion. Jason felt a world away from Fort Smith, Arkansas.

The room was dominated by a long rectangular conference table where the parties would spend the bulk of the next three days. On the far end of the table, a videographer was setting up his equipment in preparation for the depositions. He responded to someone's question in a foreign accent that Jason could not place. Next to the videographer Jason noticed a small convenience-store-type refrigerator filled with sodas and water. He was happy to see this because he drank a lot of water during legal proceedings. It was more of a nervous habit than a need for hydration. Some attorneys nervously tapped their pencils or fidgeted in their chairs, but Jason's vice was drinking water, and a lot of it.

All conversations were cut short when Bob DuPuy, Chief Operating Officer of Major League Baseball, entered the conference room and asked everyone to take a seat. DuPuy, in essence, laid out the ground rules for the depositions. He slowly walked to the far side of the conference room and leaned against a window while the dark clouds outside rolled over his head. It made for an ominous picture. DuPuy described the procedures for the depositions and the general protocol for the meetings. He said he wanted to make certain there was no confusion about the depositions and what the parties had scheduled for that week.

The preliminary discussions seemed standard enough, but before he returned to his office, DuPuy stated emphatically that he did not want to hear anything about Cuba during the proceeding or anything about Cuban players, other than what would pertain to Michel Hernández. As he walked out the door, he ended by saying, "I will be down the hall and will rule on any evidentiary issues."

DuPuy's remarks particularly grabbed Jason's attention. He thought that they were directed more to him and the documents he had already produced than to anyone else. If he could not bring up Cuba or other Cuban players, how was he going to introduce the mysterious letters into evidence? Those letters contained information on several Cuban players. This was a key piece of evidence, necessary to call into question the methods of conducting business in the international market. Now, just before the depositions were about to begin, Jason had to rethink his strategy. Fortunately, Blakeley's deposition was not until Friday, so he had two days to decide how to proceed.

Once the interpreter and Señor Ricalde were both sworn in, Rabin opened the deposition by asking Ricalde about his education background. Ricalde responded by stating that he had a "primary" school education. Rabin asked whether "primary" was equal to a university in the United States.

Ricalde said, "No. Lower."

"High school?" Rabin asked.

Again Ricalde responded, "No. Lower."

After several more questions regarding his level of education, Ricalde appeared to become annoyed and stated that he had "life experience" instead of a formal education. Ricalde must have felt in his part of the world and in his situation, real-world experience meant more than book smarts.

Rabin then moved on to questions regarding Ricalde's professional career. Ricalde purchased the Yucatan Lions baseball team in 1994 after amassing a sizeable net worth through his ownership of a chain of thirteen supermarkets throughout his region in Mexico. Ricalde had owned the chain of Super Más supermarkets for twenty-five years but had just recently leased them to another corporation.

After nearly an hour of questions about Ricalde's life, Rabin finally moved into questions related to the case. One exhibit he presented to Ricalde was a copy of the working agreement between the Yucatan Lions and the New York Yankees written in English. Rabin continually asked Ricalde questions regarding the agreement. Ricalde appeared to be evasive in his answers, which frustrated Rabin. Since Ricalde could not read English, how was he expected to answer questions about the document? The only information offered by Ricalde was that the document did contain his signature, and if it contained his signature, he stated that the document must be authentic. This was yet another glimpse into the trusting nature of the man and his culture.

Rabin asked, "Did there come a time that the Yankees cancelled the working agreement with the Lions?"

"I think that what happened was that the contract expired," Ricalde replied through the interpreter.

"And it wasn't renewed by the Yankees?"

"They did not renovate it. It was not renovated," Ricalde said.

"Does he mean renewed? It was not renewed?" Rabin asked the interpreter.

"Yes," the interpreter said.

"I just want to make sure," Rabin said, "Do you know who at the Yankees made the decision not to renew it?"

"The reason I don't know, but when it did expire, the agreement, then we had a better offer from the San Diego

Padres, and we started to work with the San Diego Padres,"
Ricalde answered.

Rabin asked, "Do you know whether Gordon Blakeley
was opposed to renewing this agreement with the Lions?"

"No."

"Were you unhappy when the Yankees decided not to
renew this?"

"No, no. The thing was -- no, no. I was not unhappy."

"Did you think that the Lions were losing some prestige
by having a contract with a team as notable as the Yankees
cancel a contract?" Rabin asked.

"I can't answer that with just one word. If he wants it, I
can explain it," Ricalde said.

"Sure. It seems to me a simple yes or no, but...?"

"Yeah. Well, then, ask the question again, please."

"Could you read it?" Rabin asked the stenographer.

The stenographer read from her laptop and said,
"Question: Did you think that the Lions were losing some
prestige by having a contract with a team as notable as the
Yankees cancel a contract?"

Jason interrupted, "I'll object to the extent that we don't
understand what a team of the type of the New York Yankees
is. If you qualify that, then I'll let him answer."

"Did you understand the question?" Rabin asked
Ricalde.

"Yes, but the Yankees did not cancel the contract."

"Fair enough. The same question, did you feel you were losing prestige when the Yankees didn't renew the contract?" Rabin asked.

"No," Ricalde responded.

Rabin moved on to another line of questioning and asked, "Ricalde, I understand that you wouldn't be able to read the English in this Bill of Particulars, but I'm going to walk through it with you and make sure that I fully understand your answers to these questions."

"Okay."

"The first question is to identify the person who typed the Agreement. And by Agreement, I mean the agreement that has been marked as Exhibit 6," Rabin asked, referring to the Hernández contract between the Yankees and Lions.

"The person, Jose Rivera Ancona."

"And he's the general manager of the Yucatan Lions?"

"Mm-hmm," Ricalde mumbled.

"And that's what it states in the document. The second question – and I'm going to ask you to translate the full question, state the date, time and place, including address the alleged Agreement was typed. And the answer as read here is, on or about November 21, 1996, Calle 50 No. 406. Is that answer truthful?"

"Yes."

"And what is at this address?"

"Calle 50 406, that's the offices of the club," Ricalde answered, referring to the offices of the Yucatan Lions.

"Do you know what time of day the agreement was typed?"

"No, I don't remember. Possibly in the afternoon."

"And why do you say possibly the afternoon?"

"Well, because everything was done in one day, and I'm not sure. It was a long time ago."

"When you say everything was done in one day, what are you referring to?" Rabin asked.

"To check the player. We reached the terms of this. It was signed. And that's where it ended. The player was... the Yankees were in charge of the player. The player stayed as a guest in the hotel, but we had nothing more to do with that."

"So the Yankees checked the player and the agreement was signed, and this all occurred in one day?"

"Yes."

"And that date was November 21, 1996?"

"I'm not sure it was on the 21st of November, because of the situation of the ball player," Ricalde answered.

"I thought you just said that the contract was signed on November 21."

"What I said was around November 21."

"Do you believe that to be the date this contract was signed?"

"I think not. I'm not sure why, but I think it was, like, not convenient for... to put the date on this contract. Because we had to look after certain aspects because of the illegal situation in which the ball player was in Mexico."

"You previously have said, both in this document and this morning that the agreement was typed November 21, 1996. Is that correct or incorrect?"

"That it was written the day we signed it."

"The contract was signed the same day it was typed up?"

"That the contract was signed the same date that it was typed, yes."

"And that day was on or about November 21, 1996?"

"About that... around that day," Ricalde said.

"And you say that because of the illegal situation of the player?"

"When I'm saying the player, you know, I'm saying illegal because he was a Cuban."

"Okay," Rabin said.

"He didn't have a passport. He had nothing. He had no documents."

"Why did that affect the day the contract was typed and signed?"

"Because we wanted to disassociate ourselves, at least as far as I'm concerned, because the Mexican police was looking for him."

"Do you remember when I asked you if the Yankees checked the player and the player was signed, and it all occurred in one day?"

"Yes."

"And do you remember that you said the answer to that was yes?"

"Yes."

"So did the Yankees see the player try out on November 21, 1996?"

"No, that day... that day they saw the player. I'm not saying they didn't see him on the 21st. I've always said around November 21."

"And before you said that because of the illegal situation of the player, I want to understand what you were saying. How did the legal situation of the player affect when this agreement was signed?" Rabin asked.

"Because of the situation as on a personal basis, because the illegal situation of the player."

"So what impact did that have on the dates?"

"At the end there was no impact. Because they didn't... because they didn't arrest Michel. He left Mexico. I don't know how. So possibly afterwards, you know, there was -- afterwards, you know, I didn't want to be involved in a situation of immigration."

"Explain to me, if you could, how the legal situation of the player delayed signing the contract?"

"The signature was not delayed, because it was signed the same day. Right now, as we're sitting here, I don't even remember the reason for why we weren't putting the date – we didn't want to put the date. It was because not only me, but the Yankees, we both knew that we were signing up a person who was illegal."

Senor Ricalde's testimony was as forthright and telling as any witness Jason had observed. Ricalde understood the circumstances surrounding the contract, and was honest, and secure enough in himself to reveal in the presence of the Commissioner's personnel the true nature of this transaction. Ricalde's honesty made it clear that, in keeping with Jason's strategy, he was going to lay all cards out on the table.

"When this agreement was originally typed up, and before it was signed, was the date on the agreement?"

"I don't remember."

"So it's probable that the date, which appears on the last line of [the agreement], was on the document before Jorge Oquendo signed it?"

"It's probable."

"But you don't know for sure?"

"Well, because so much time has gone by it's probable, and because of the way I do the agreements I probably dictated it and made it in black and white and then afterwards it was signed."

"And you're saying that it's possible that this last line, referring to November 21, 1996, was not there when the document was signed?"

"No."

"That's not possible?"

"Most probably it was all there when Oquendo signed it."

"My question is, are you certain, as you sit here today, that the document signed by Oquendo was final when he signed it?"

"Yes."

"Is there a different date that you think it could have been?"

"Yes, from what I said earlier. Because of the situation of the player, that we were both trying to protect ourselves, and possibly that's why we dealt with a later date than the one on -- on the signing date."

"So what you're saying is you may have signed a document with an incorrect date on it?"

"No, no, no. What I'm saying is that it's most probable that it was signed on a date different than the one here, but both parties agreed upon that."

"Do you know an approximate date on which you think it actually was signed, if it wasn't signed on the 21st?"

"Right now I'm beginning to remember what the main reasons were. The main reason was that the people who were from the Yankees could not tie in the date that the person was in Merida with the signature of the date of the contract, because they didn't want it known that they were in Merida. That's one of the situations, since it didn't affect the date."

"Do you know approximately when you think it actually was signed?"

"Of what I am sure is that it was before this date," Ricalde said.

"When you say people from the New York Yankees wanted it signed on a different day, what people are you referring to?"

"Well, of the two people, Mr. Gordon Blakeley, and of Oquendo. I have to tell you that since the contact with the

Yankees was made by Mr. Carlos Paz, representative in Mexico, paid by the Yankees, he asked me that it be in total secret because of the baseball rules. It was absolutely forbidden for the clubs to try to sign, especially Cuban players."

"Was it illegal for the Lions?"

"For the Lions it couldn't be legal."

"Why not?" Rabin asked.

"Because a ballplayer who doesn't have documents, we can't get a working visa, to be able to have him on the club's roster. It's obvious that if that ball player had had a working visa it would have been the property of the club and the worth would have been different."

"Did Mr. Blakeley specifically – are you alleging that Mr. Blakeley specifically told you that he wanted to predate this agreement a date earlier than November 21st?"

"No."

"So what's your basis for saying that he wanted to date it before November 21?"

"The date we agreed upon with Jorge Oquendo."

"Not with Carlos Paz?"

"No. With respect to the agreement Mr. Paz didn't tell me anything. What Mr. Paz told me, when he confirmed to me that they were arriving the next day, Mr. Gordon (Blakeley) and Jorge Oquendo, that since they were executives of a very high level, on no account did they want any press; on no account did they want them to know that they had been even in Merida checking this ballplayer out."

"But Paz didn't tell you anything about the dating of this agreement?"

"No. No, not him. The one who told me was Jorge Oquendo. Jorge Oquendo. It was with Jorge Oquendo that we agreed upon all of this. Jorge Oquendo would ask somebody, I don't know whom, and before signing…before signing, then he went up to his room, I imagine, to see if they agreed about this. What they were anticipating was that in a certain moment they could deny having been in Merida on the 21st, because of the problem that they could have with the organized baseball. That was the reason. And on another side was that it did… was convenient for me because I was covered by that."

"How were you covered?"

"Well, how things are… how things are protected in Mexico."

"So you were concerned that you were violating the law, and by dating it November 21st you thought that might help avoid detection?"

Jason interrupted, "Objection to the use of the term law versus rules. Major League rules versus law."

"Okay," Rabin said, "What were you being protected from, Mexican law, baseball rules?"

"Of the legal thing in Mexico. And also the fear of the consequences it could have in organized baseball, of which the Yankees people didn't know very well."

"Who did you speak to about this agreement with the Yankees?"

"Jorge Oquendo."

"Not with Mr. Blakeley?"

"No."

"Not with Mr. Newman?"

"No."

"And not with any of the general partners of the New York Yankees?"

"With nobody. Not with Newman, with Blakeley. I greeted him when he came to the park."

"Your sole basis for the Yankees' views in connection with this agreement comes from your discussions with Jorge Oquendo?"

"Yes."

Rabin then asked about why the contract was notarized and why other contracts with the Yankees were not notarized.

Ricalde simply answered, "Because of the illegality of the contract, it could not be registered with Major League Baseball therefore I wanted it to at least be notarized."

"So the notary didn't care that he was notarizing a document with a date that was sometime after the date of the notarization?"

"Because what was asked of him was to attest as to the people who were signing the document."

"And he issued his seal even though the date listed on the document was sometime in the future?"

"That's it. Because for us, and I'm going to repeat it again, what was important for us was to authenticate the signatures of the people to make it a valid document."

"What was written here by the notary was inaccurate?"

"That's it. With respect to the date."

"So just to have this right. We have a document here that is – an agreement that is notarized, and the notary's own certification is incorrect? That's the testimony?"

"Yes."

Next Rabin moved on to the events directly surrounding the signing of the contract. Ricalde began to walk the attorneys through the timeline of the case. He described how he learned of Hernández' defection, though he would not disclose the names of those who introduced him to Hernández. Those who helped Hernández defect were Cuban, and for reasons of safety Ricalde did not want to disclose their identity. At least one of those involved still lived in Cuba, and to be accused of helping a fellow Cuban defect would certainly mean imprisonment, if not death.

He described his recollection of events, how he called Carlos Paz regarding Hernández and that the next day Oquendo and Gordon Blakeley were in Mexico to meet with himself and Hernández. The Yankees attorneys spent a considerable amount of time questioning Ricalde about the timeframe and events surrounding the signing of what they termed the "alleged contract."

Ricalde did just as Jason requested; he answered questions forthrightly and did not deviate from his story. He made certain to point out that he felt he had adhered to the working agreement by contacting the Yankees first regarding Hernández defection. Even in the face of a possible illegal act, Ricalde kept his word.

Shortly after noon a lunch break was called. Jason, Ricalde and Eddie Diaz dined at a restaurant directly across the street from the Commissioner's office. Oquendo was not with the group, since his deposition was not until the next day. Oquendo, who spent a large part of his youth in Brooklyn before moving back to Puerto Rico with his family, had taken the day to walk across the Brooklyn Bridge to visit his old neighborhood and some friends who remained there.

At lunch Jason was hurried. He did not even look at the menu offered to him by the waiter but ordered a salad. Ricalde and Diaz, on the other hand, took full advantage of the break and ordered an array of what the restaurant offered. The conversation, as it had at breakfast, drifted into a casual one, which unnerved Jason. He wanted to keep Ricalde focused on the depositions. Jason knew Ricalde would rather be anywhere other than New York being grilled by Yankee attorneys, but they were nearly halfway through Ricalde's deposition, and Jason knew the importance of not straying too far from the subject. Ricalde and Diaz eventually relented, and the three reviewed the morning's testimony. So far, everything had gone relatively smoothly, but Jason knew that might not be the case for the afternoon.

"Look, so far, so good," Jason said to Ricalde, "Just keep answering questions the way you have been and be careful not to elaborate unless you're asked to do so."

They continued to go over his testimony until it was time to return to the depositions.

During the afternoon testimony, Ricalde finished his recollection of events and the Yankees' counsel began to test his story trying to find any inconsistencies or any way to impeach Ricalde. They asked many of the same questions only in a different form. Ricalde did not fall for their strategy. He was calm throughout. If he did not understand a question, he would take the time to get verification from Jason. He may not have worked at the same speed as the attorneys, but Ricalde was just as thorough. Each question and answer had to be translated, which made Ricalde's deposition much longer than expected.

Yankees' counsel questioned the amount that was agreed upon for Hernández. They argued that half a million dollars was far too much for a player of Hernández' talents, even if he was Cuban.

Ricalde responded, "We started talking with Oquendo. Oquendo started saying that they liked the player, but they couldn't have money authorized to give me, and tried to find a way. Where in reality they didn't have to put in anything, and they were only going to give the money if he reached the forty-man roster, with them. Through the Yankees. And that's why right now it could look like an exaggerated amount, when in reality in those days what they were paying for the other players who had deserted, based on the parameters that they were getting paid, I think that they thought it was a very good deal, because if Hernández had not reached the forty-man roster they wouldn't have to pay anything."

Rabin asked what happened after the contract was signed.

Ricalde responded, "Once we reached an agreement, I gave the instructions about how it was going to be typed, and then I had the opportunity to listen to a conversation that the ballplayer would be taken out by somebody named Dominguez. Then at that point I thought they were talking about Ken Dominguez, who is a coach, whom the Yankees sent, but apparently the person who took him out was a person with the last name of Dominguez, whom I do not know. Nor do I know when they took him out, nor through where did they take him out."

"And who did you overhear talking about this Dominguez?" Rabin asked.

"Well, with the only one I was talking to, Jorge Oquendo," Ricalde said.

"And then was business concluded for the night at that time?"

"Everything was finished, and we haven't talked about the case anymore, because, you know, we lost sight of this ballplayer."

"Was there anything done the next day, in terms of meetings with the Yankee personnel?" Rabin asked.

"No. I didn't even find out when they left Merida. I didn't even find out when they left, or even when the ballplayer left. And the main reason is that Merida is such a small city, and they don't... they didn't want anybody to know that they were there, in Merida. So after the day that we signed I never again saw them in Merida."

"Were the Yankees the only club that you approached about Michel Hernández being in Merida?" Rabin asked.

"It was the only one. But I'm not sure that the people who were managing him before did not contact other clubs. And I only offered him to the Yankees, and if we hadn't reached this agreement, which then frankly was not very favorable, the only thing I had was I had an interest in was to do it with the Yankees, because I felt that the Yankees, what really… they were interested out of Yucatan was the geographic location that we had versus Cuba, and that they always showed us the interest to get Cuban ballplayers. That was confirmed when I spoke to them before, through their scout, Carlos Paz. He tells them and asks them if they're interested in this kid, Michel. When Carlos Paz says yes to me, that they would arrive next day then I gave the instructions to people who were looking at him to take Michel Hernández to Merida."

"Had you previously referred any other Cuban players to the Yankees?"

"Not exactly, but they had given me names, because they had the information of the important ball players in Cuba. Even the detail of the dates when they went out to compete."

"Did the Yankees ever demand an exclusive opportunity to view Michel Hernández?"

"No, no."

"Did you ever tell the Yankees they were getting an exclusive look at Michel Hernández?"

"No. No, neither the Mexican players. This was a very separate operation from the agreement. Very separate from the agreement. It was only that when this situation arose, the only club that I offered to was the Yankees because we had a relationship. They could have said I'm not interested and it would have ended there. They had no obligation."

"Mr. Ricalde, did you ever discuss the agreement with the Yankees after you... after it was signed?" Rabin asked.

"Never. Once in a while I asked Jorge, Jorge Oquendo, and this guy said he didn't know anything about it. He didn't know what had happened, and he disappeared for a long time, like something two years he didn't appear in reserves or anything like that."

"Michel Hernández disappeared?"

"Michel Hernández, yes."

"So you occasionally asked Jorge Oquendo what was happening with Michel Hernández?"

"Maybe during the following year. Afterwards the agreement with the Yankees was over, and I lost contact completely with the Yankees, because we already had an agreement with the San Diego Padres, and I didn't have..."

Rabin interrupted, "You didn't have any contact with the Yankees?"

"No information. No information."

"Now when you were speaking to Jorge Oquendo, was that after he had left the New York Yankees?"

"Yes. We kept on talking, because we were exporting Mexican players."

"When was this?"

"We continued exporting, well, it's been like three or four years. First he was with Cincinnati. Especially after 2001, when we no longer had any agreement with any club. So once in a while we invited him to come out for the trials that we would hold in Yucatan, but he didn't go even once to Yucatan."

"Mr. Oquendo, this is?"

"Mr. Oquendo. Shall I comment about the trip?" Ricalde asked.

"Let him ask the questions," Jason injected, referring to Rabin.

"What trip are you referring to?" Rabin asked.

"That after this operation that we had, the interest of the Yankees was so great on the Cubans, I think that precisely in that year there were the most important years when the Cuban players were on top, and the major league clubs were desperate to get any Cuban player that would come out. So at that time we had operations in Cuba through the Empacadora de Carnes Frias that we had in Yucatan, the frozen meat company that is managed by Carlos Canto. And he made contacts in Cuba."

"Who is 'he'?"

"Carlos Canto. Carlos Canto. He's my partner."

"Okay. Did you ever speak to Mr. Blakeley after November 1996?"

"No."

"Did you ever speak to Mark Newman after November 1996?"

"No."

"Did you become aware in 1998 that the Yankees had signed Michel Hernández?"

"I don't remember. I don't remember."

"At some point did you learn that the Yankees had signed Michel Hernández?"

"Yes. I think yes, that I did find out, and then suddenly he disappeared again."

"When you learned that the Yankees had signed Michel Hernández, did you take steps to remind anybody about this agreement, anybody at the Yankees?"

"When I saw that he reached the forty-man roster?" Ricalde asked.

"No, just whenever you learned that he had been signed by the Yankees."

"No. No."

"Any reason why not?"

"The fact that he was hired under contract for class A or… or Double or Triple-A. If it wasn't the forty-man roster there was no reason to."

"Weren't you nervous that the Yankees were going to forget about the agreement, that the agreement existed, since it was signed in 1996?"

"Well, truly I didn't… I didn't think about it. Truly I didn't think about it. You know, the Yankees being one of the most serious organizations in baseball. I didn't think about it, and he didn't let me finish talking about Cuba, that had… that was related to this."

"That's fine. It was a rambling answer that I just didn't think needed to be completed," Rabin said then continued, "Okay. Are there any contracts, as you sit here today, that Oquendo signed his signature on for the New York Yankees?"

"About players' contracts?"

"Yes."

"No."

Rabin leaned back in his chair and said, "Subject to a right to redirect for Mr. Browning, I think I'm done."

But Ricalde was not finished. He brought up another time when the Yankees had expressed interest in Cuban players. "No, the only thing related to that question, that (Oquendo) commented to me when he came back at me, when I said that he didn't have the authority to sign this, that's when he told me that he had signed many players for a lot of money. But I am… I can't attest to it."

Rabin reengaged and asked, "Did he mention any of the players that he had signed?"

"No. He didn't tell me exactly who."

"And when did he tell you this, that he had signed a lot of players for a lot of money?"

"When I called him the first time. When the lawyer called me, telling me that there were problems with the Yankees. I considered that the logical thing was that he had to clear the situation up."

"Right. I'm asking about when Mr. Oquendo told you that he had signed a lot of players for the New York Yankees."

"Well, when did he tell me? He made the comment after we had been...after this was over. We made a trip to Moncton, Canada, with the purpose of getting four Cuban players out, that we had already gotten, to desert in Moncton, Canada. On that trip Carlos Canto went with me, Jorge Oquendo, and the esquire Jean [Afterman] who is here accompanying us, and I'm only commenting this today because of the promotion, if Gordon knew about this trip or not, or Newman. But this happened after we signed this. And so then that made me think that everything was fine with the Yankees."

"Was Jean Afterman working with the Yankees at the time?"

"Jean, I think, was not working for the Yankees then. She went along with us – she went along with us, and I know that there were two buyers, I don't know whether one Japanese, one Korean, whom I never saw, but the operation could not be done because the four players who had made the commitment to get out, among the four of them was not the one whom the Japanese liked, Ismael Rodriguez. And so the Japanese, their condition was that in order to take those four, Ismael Rodriguez also had to get out."

Rabin, looking frustrated by Ricalde's response, replied, "Could I just ask, the question, which I could have read back, was when Jorge Oquendo told you he had signed a lot of players to a lot of money for the Yankees. Is there an answer anywhere in this dialogue? You seem to want to get this information on the record."

"In that occasion we had the chance to be together for three or four days."

What Señor Ricalde was doing was simply explaining why he didn't follow up with the Yankees regarding the contract for Hernández, and that making a trip with Oquendo to Canada made him think everything was still good with the Yankees – that the terms of the agreement, if Michel made the forty-man roster, would be satisfied. Simple dialogue between himself and the Yankees was enough to keep Ricalde comfortable with the situation at that time. He didn't need an attorney to review the situation. As long as they were still on speaking terms, he felt as confident as he had in any other business deals.

"He told you that he had signed a lot of players?" Rabin asked.

"Yes. And after that we never again had contact."

"And you say this was in Moncton, Canada?"

"Moncton, Canada."

"And the purchasers were a Korean and Japanese teams?"

"Yes. They were either for Korea or Japan. I'm not sure. But I never saw the buyers."

"And do you know whether Jorge Oquendo was with the Yankees at the time this took place?"

"Yes. When this happened, yes, he was with the Yankees."

"What year was it?"

"Well, maybe Jean could help," Ricalde said as he glanced towards Jean Afterman sitting across the table.

"Well, she's not testifying today, so I'm just wondering whether you know."

"Well, I think it must have been in '97. '97, yes."

"I don't have anything further," Rabin concluded.

By 5:30 that afternoon Ricalde was tired of his reputation being called into question and interjected, "I would like to make a comment. I consider myself a man of baseball. I don't come with the spirit of fighting. I come with the intention to clear up what has to be cleared up. When I was asked whether not renewing the contract with the Yankees would damage my prestige, the Yankees did not give me my prestige. I have earned that through many years of work. The least thing I want is a situation that is not aligned with the guidelines of baseball."

During Jason's cross examination, he attempted to clear up some of the questions raised by the Yankees' attorneys. Mainly, the question of whether Jorge Oquendo truly had the authority to sign the contract on behalf of the Yankees. Jason began by showing Ricalde Exhibit 2, a letter from Rudy Santin, the Yankees Coordinator for Latin American Scouting.

"Mr. Ricalde, the letter you're now looking at is a letter addressed to you from a Rudy Santin, correct?" Jason asked.

"Mm-hmm."

"And his title under his name as signed is Coordinator for Latin American scouting, correct?"

"That's it."

"Did you work with or negotiate with Mr. Santin for working agreements with the New York Yankees on behalf of the Yucatan Lions?"

"Yes. The first agreement was with Rudy Santin, yes."

"In regard to that, was it your understanding that Mr. Santin had authority to negotiate with you on behalf of the New York Yankees?"

"Correct."

"Did you ever question his authority to negotiate with you?"

"No, no, there was no doubt, because the contract went... was good and the Yankees always... they met their obligations with what we dealt with. Especially the one afterwards that was a much more complete agreement."

"So some working agreements and/or negotiations that you had with Mr. Santin actually came to fruition?"

"Yes."

"If you would turn to Exhibit 6, it's the contract."

"Yes."

"What is Mr. Oquendo's title?" Jason asked.

"Director of Scouting for Latin America."

"And that was conveyed to you, I believe your testimony was, by Carlos Paz?"

"Carlos Paz told me that Jorge Oquendo had taken over the position of Rudy Santin. Carlos Paz, the representative of the Yankees in Mexico."

"If you negotiated with Rudy Santin and Mr. Oquendo took the position of Mr. Santin, would you have any reason to doubt Mr. Oquendo's authority to negotiate with you?"

"If I negotiated with Santin, what?" Ricalde asked.

Jason continued, "From what Carlos Paz told you about Jorge Oquendo, did you have any reason to believe he didn't have authority to negotiate with you?"

"No. No, especially with Gordon [Blakeley] in front of me, he told me to negotiate with Oquendo."

"When negotiating with Mr. Oquendo, were you negotiating with Mr. Oquendo individually or with the New York Yankees?"

"The contract, the agreement in the first part of it... it starts out by saying that we're going to negotiate with Mr. Oquendo representing the Yankees, and the one who is here representing the Leones of Yucatan. Therefore, everything that is expressed below and is signed at the end of this cannot be declarations on a personal basis." Jason wanted Ricalde to explain that while negotiating with Oquendo, Ricalde understood he was negotiating with the Yankees organization, not the individual. Whether Oquendo actually held the title he had was relatively immaterial because the title was conveyed to Ricalde, and Ricalde was of the understanding that the scout had the requisite authority to negotiate on the Yankees' behalf.

Rabin had more questions for Ricalde on his redirect. He again attempted to get Ricalde to disclose the names of those involved in Hernández' defection. "You said that if you recovered $500,000 you would have to pay part of it to the people who got him out. Did you mean to the people that got Mr. Hernández out of Cuba?" Rabin asked.

"That's it. The people who were involved to take him out of Cuba. In Cuba and in Mexico."

"If you don't recover this amount, how will you satisfy any obligations to the people who got him out of Cuba?"

"If I don't recover the amount, I will have to show them that I didn't recover it. And that I don't have the obligation to give them the money either. Because we're partners in what we're going to receive, and since you're asking me the question, to clear that up even more…"

Rabin interrupted, "I just want to say before you clear up this question, if this is not on point I'm going to cut you down before your… because a lot of times you want to say you want to clear up something and you go off the deep end. So if you have something to clear up this question, by all means offer it."

"Well, it does have to do with a question that he already asked and that I didn't answer. Because as things are coming back, I would like to answer why. Why I don't want to give him the name of the people involved."

"Okay," Rabin said.

"Because they are Cuban, who are in Cuba. And that it would be even mortal for them, because to be involved in a matter such as this, it is a very serious crime in Cuba. They have family members who live in Yucatan, and definitively, that is the reason."

The gravity of this testimony was not lost on those present in the conference room. It also opened Jason's eyes a bit wider to the serious nature of this segment of the business. Jason could only think of other Cuban defectors who played professional baseball in the United States and the circumstances of their respective defections. The human element behind these transactions was put aside in Jason's mind, but hearing Ricalde speak in this environment of the actual workings in this industry awakened Jason.

Rabin continued, "You testified that if Mr. Hernández didn't make the forty-man with the New York Yankees no monies would be owed under this agreement?"

"There wouldn't be. And I, yes, I'm aware that if he's not... if it's not valuable for the Yankees, it's not valuable for anyone."

Around eight o'clock that evening, during a break, Jason walked down the hall to use the restroom where he ran into Rich Rabin and Ed Burns.

Within earshot of Burns, Jason asked Rabin, "How much longer is this going to go?" Jason explained that the length of the proceeding was wearing his client down. Ricalde was not a young man and Jason felt, at that point, the Yankees' counsel was leading Ricalde in circles, trying unsuccessfully to catch him in a contradiction.

Ed Burns, who overheard the exchange, agreed. He felt it was time to end for the day. Everything Ricalde knew had been said and it was on videotape. Jason hoped that if there was need for further meetings, the videos would suffice. He did not want Ricalde to have to fly back from Mexico again just to rehash the same story.

It was dark outside when the depositions were suspended late that evening. Everyone was exhausted. Since the rain had stopped, Jason and his team walked back to their hotel. He didn't realize just how close the hotel was until he noticed the walk back was shorter than the cab ride over.

Somewhat beleaguered, Jason rejoined Ricalde in his room where he ordered beer from room service. Jason sipped on a Heineken while he debriefed Ricalde. Before long, Jason could see by Señor Ricalde's exhausted expression that he was tired, so to give Ricalde some much needed rest, Jason returned to his room to prepare for the next day. Tomorrow would be Oquendo's turn and Jason was anxious to see Oquendo face his former employer. He knew Oquendo was probably ready to get some answers as well. Oquendo had to feel as if he had been used as an expendable middle man. Neither Oquendo nor Ricalde felt they were in the wrong and both deserved to know why they were accused of being part of what the Yankees termed a 'shakedown.'

CHAPTER 6

"It's unbelievable how much you don't know about the game you've been playing all your life."
- Mickey Mantle

Thursday morning, September 9th, Jason's group ate breakfast together again in the hotel. Señor Ricalde and Eddie Diaz were to fly back home later that morning. Once again, the case was barely discussed, but Ricalde thanked Jason for his efforts in the case and wished him luck for the remainder of the week.

After seeing Ricalde and Diaz off, Jason and Oquendo set out for the Commissioner's office. The weather was much more cooperative, so the two decided to walk. Jason was pulling an Oxbox, a miniature dolly, stacked full of documents. The Oxbox was new, but with the beating it was taking on the rough streets of Manhattan, it already appeared to be well-used. The Oxbox looked the way Jason felt.

They arrived at the Commissioner's office and were put through the same tedious security check as the day before followed by the thirty-one story ride in the elevator. That day, there was no wait in the lobby. Ed Burns met them at the front desk and escorted them immediately to the conference room. Without Ricalde and the translators, the room was less crowded. Unlike the previous morning, there was little conversation. Jason sensed more tension among the participants. He wasn't certain if Ricalde's long day of testimony had tired everyone or if the Yankees' counsel was hesitant or reluctant to hear Oquendo's testimony. Either way, the participants were relatively silent during their preparations and the deposition began on time.

Oquendo was seated at the head of the table with Jason directly to his left. Across from Jason, and to Oquendo's right, sat Rich Rabin. Next to Rabin sat Michelle Burg, followed by Jean Afterman, and Lonn Trost. Ed Burns, Vice President of Baseball Operations, sat three seats to the left of Jason and was already starting to take copious notes. Oquendo's deposition began with each person present stating their name for the record. "Counsel, please state your appearances for the record," the videographer asked.

"Richard Rabin, New York Yankees."

"Jean Afterman, New York Yankees."

"Lonn Trost, New York Yankees."

"Michele Burg for the New York Yankees."

"Jason Browning for the Yucatan Lions."

Jason felt outnumbered, no doubt about it.

Oquendo swiveled back and forth in his chair as his deposition began. Just as he had with Ricalde, Rabin began by inquiring about Oquendo's education and unlike Ricalde, Oquendo had a high school education. Oquendo was then asked about what he did following high school. Oquendo stated that in 1981 he signed to play in the Oakland A's organization where he stayed for three years before being signed to the Detroit Tigers organization.

By 1987, Oquendo was out as a professional baseball player, without any time in the Major Leagues. Later that year, he began to work for Fed Ex in his home country of Puerto Rico. In 1994, while he worked for Fed Ex, he also worked as a part-time scout for the Yankees. His position at Fed Ex allowed him the flexibility to choose which days of the week he wished to work. He worked a thirty to thirty-five hour week, Monday through Thursday, and then he'd scout for the Yankees Friday through Sunday. By 1996, Oquendo moved up in the scouting ranks and was positioned to become the Coordinator of Latin American Scouting when the current coordinator, Rudy Santin, was fired.

Rabin asked Oquendo about the time he encountered Ricalde at the 2002 Major League Baseball Winter Meetings in Nashville. This was the first time the two had seen each other since the Hernández contract was signed.

Oquendo said, "To be honest with you, I didn't want to look him in the face. Because, at that time, we didn't do the right thing to that gentleman."

Rabin inquired as to how Ricalde got in touch with Oquendo, and Oquendo answered that he received the call on his cell phone. Rabin then asked how Ricalde came to have Oquendo's cell phone number. Rabin was possibly trying to establish a pre-existing link between Ricalde and Oquendo, but any questions surrounding this were quickly answered when Oquendo said, "Everybody's got my cell phone number, it's on my (business) card."

Oquendo took Rabin back through the phone call he had with Ricalde shortly after Hernández made the Yankees' forty-man roster. "Ricalde says, Mr. Oquendo, Michel Hernández is on the forty-man roster and I think the agreement that we made, you know, on Michel, when he gets on the forty-man roster, of $500,000. I think your guys got to pay me. I told him, 'Mr. Ricalde, excuse me a minute, I'm not with the New York Yankees no more. I am with the Cincinnati Reds. But just give me time and let me see. Let me look at the situation.' To be honest with you, he caught me out of the blue."

Oquendo continued, "So I immediately did – I called Gordon Blakeley. I called the office, I called his cell… he never returned my call. I told him, Gordon, we got an issue here with the Yucatan Lions and I need you to call me ASAP. Call me as soon as possible. He never called me."

"How long after receiving the call from Mr. Ricalde did you call Mr. Blakeley?" Rabin asked.

"Hanging up with him I called Gordon."

"You left him a message to the effect he should call you as soon as possible?"

"Um-hum, um-hum, and his cell phone."

"And Mr. Blakeley didn't get back to you?"

"Not at all."

"Did you call him again?"

"I called him two times, he don't respond. I guess he don't want to talk to me."

"So you didn't want to call him again?"

"No. My next step was I called Jean Afterman and I said we got a problem."

"What was the problem that you related to Jean?"

"That I tried to get to Gordon Blakeley and he doesn't want to call me. And I explained to Jean Afterman the problem."

"The basis that you said Gordon didn't want to speak to you, that you left him a message and he didn't call you back?"

"Absolutely, and I said that."

"Was there any other basis that Gordon didn't want to talk to you other than he hadn't returned the call?"

"Hadn't returned the call."

"You said to Jean, we have a problem?" Rabin asked.

"I said, Jean, me and Gordon we made a contract with Ricalde from Mexico and Michel is on the forty-man roster and I think we got a big problem here. So Jean told me, Jorge..."

"Can I ask you, why did you think there was a problem?" Rabin interrupted.

"I guess if I call you and tell you we made a deal with a Cuban player, when it is a Cuban player, it is a problem. You don't want to deal with Cuban players."

"Right. Did you think it was a problem that the Yankees were going to have to pay some money under the contract or was the contract itself a problem? I don't understand what the problem was."

"I think that Gordon didn't want to face the problem that he had to pay the money."

"What was your basis for saying Gordon didn't want to face the problem?"

"If I call you twice and tell you about the situation and you don't call me, I am assuming that you don't want to hear nothing about it."

"How soon after you called Gordon did you call Jean?"

"After two days, I gave him two days because sometimes you got to give the guy some credibility because sometimes he is traveling."

"Right. All kinds of reasons why people don't return phone calls?"

"You can be wherever you at. At nighttime, where you go, you check your voice mail."

"You can," Rabin said.

"Everybody does, especially when you work for the Yankees."

"So your testimony is Gordon Blakeley checks his cell phone messages every night?"

"Yes."

"What was your basis for that?"

"When you are in a position like that, a lot of things are running. When you are a director, if you don't answer your phone, some other scout can call you, says, 'I just saw a guy throwing 96 (miles per hour).' If you don't answer your phone, you just missed out on that."

"I understand. Are you personally aware that Gordon Blakeley has a personal habit of checking his cell phone messages?"

"Yes."

"What did Ms. Afterman say to you?"

"Jean told me, 'Jorge, do you got the documents?' I said, 'Yes.' She said, 'Fax it to me.' I said, 'No, no, Gordon has to have his copy. Tell Gordon to give you his copy.'"

"Did you explain to Jean what the terms of the contract were?"

"Yes."

"To your knowledge, did Jean Afterman have any prior knowledge of the existence of the alleged contract before you called her?"

"I have no idea."

"Did you explain to Jean the particular circumstances surrounding how the contract was entered?"

"Yes. I said, 'Jean, me and Gordon, we made a contract that if Michel ever gets to the forty-man roster, New York Yankees have to pay five hundred thousand dollars to Gustavo (Ricalde),' and I told Jean, 'Let's try to fix this because I don't want to be where I am at right now. Things are going to get ugly here. So let's try to fix this.' And I went beyond. I spoke to Cashman in person at the winter meeting in Nashville. I also told Cashman. I tried to fix everything, everything, before sitting where I am at right now."

"Did you have any knowledge when you called Jean whether the Yankees were going or were not going to pay the $500,000 that was allegedly owed?"

"I can't answer that for you."

"I guess I just don't understand why you think there was a problem. If the Yankees paid the money, would you be sitting where you are right now?"

"No."

"Why did you think… you seemed to have jumped to a conclusion and I am trying to figure out what was the basis of your jumping to the conclusion that they weren't going to pay?"

"I know Gordon Blakeley. I know when things top out, international things, he don't want no part of it."

"You were confident when you called Jean that the Yankees were not going to pay this money?"

"Yes, because I have worked with Jean in the past and we had a great relationship. I assumed we did."

"What was Jean's reaction?"

"Jean was very calm. She say, 'Jorge, I will return your call, let me investigate,' and to the day, Jean never returned my call either."

"She asked you for a copy and you said you would not fax her a copy?"

"That's correct."

"Why wouldn't you fax her a copy?"

"I won't because I don't trust nobody when you do international work."

Rabin then asked who else Oquendo had talked to about the situation. Oquendo said he had spoken about it with Brian Cashman during the 2002 Winter Meeting in Nashville.

"Before we get into Cashman, did you speak to Ricalde again after speaking with Jean (Afterman)?" Rabin asked.

"No," Oquendo responded, "When you owe somebody five hundred thousand dollars, you don't want to talk to nobody."

"Did you think you owed Ricalde five hundred thousand dollars?"

"Not me, the Yankees."

"So there's no other communication, after the call to Jean, until you see Mr. Cashman in Nashville?"

"That's correct."

"And what did you say to Cashman?" Rabin asked.

"I asked him if he had a couple of minutes and he said, 'Sure Jorge,' which he's a great individual, great person. We sat down and I said, 'Cashman we got some problems here. We got a player we signed unlegal, a Cuban player, and now Gordon (Blakeley) doesn't want to show up. I spoke to Gordon about it. I spoke to Jean about it and nobody wants to respond on this.'"

Rabin jumped on this, "Can we back up? You did speak to Gordon about it?"

"I left him a message," Oquendo said.

"Okay, so you didn't speak to him about it?"

"Right."

"Did you tell Cashman that you had spoken to Gordon about it?"

"Yes. Left him a message."

"And again, your deduction that there was a big problem was the fact that you never received a call back from Gordon and you had this conversation with Jean and hadn't heard back from her?"

"Yes, that's correct."

Rabin switched gears, "So did you speak with Ricalde at these Winter Meetings?"

"Yes, it was, 'Hey, how you doing?' He said he was working on getting an attorney and I said, 'You do what you have to do. I respect that.' That was about it."

Rabin then asked why Oquendo was so interested in the case since he was no longer a Yankee when Hernández made the Yankees forty-man roster. Oquendo said, "Because it was a lot of unlegal stuff that was out there that I didn't want to get in to, like sitting here right now. We did a lot of unlegal stuff. It was not proper and when things like that come out, it's not healthy for the New York Yankees or for Major League Baseball… and also for me."

Rabin then asked about the dialogue between Oquendo and Jason after Jason was hired to represent the Yucatan club, "When did you learn that an arbitration had been filed in this matter?"

"Jason called me," Oquendo responded.

"When did Jason call you?"

"One to two months after the meeting in Nashville, I got a call from Jason. He was a representative of the Yucatan Lions."

"What did he say?"

"He asked me about the situation, just like you're doing and I responded to him just like I'm doing to you."

"Had you ever spoken to Jason any time before you received this call?"

"I never knew him." With a grin Oquendo continued, "He's from Arkansas."

"I'm sorry?" Rabin asked.

"He's from Arkansas," Oquendo repeated in a tone that suggested "Why would I know anybody from Arkansas? Does anybody know anyone from Arkansas?"

An eruption of laughter was heard in the background followed by a brief pause while the participants gathered themselves.

Next Rabin questioned Oquendo about the mysterious documents that Oquendo had provided to Jason.

"I gave him some copies of some contracts of players that I had signed."

Rabin asked, "Did you provide him with any other kinds of documents?"

"Yes, I did."

"What else did you provide him with?"

"I provided him with a letter that got to my house. The funny thing about that letter, it didn't have a return address on it."

"Who was the letter from?"

"I have no idea. It didn't have a return address."

"Did you look at the text of the letter?"

"Yes."

"And was it a letter from someone to someone?"

"It was a couple of pages of something of Gordon Blakeley's."

"And you have no idea who sent it to you?" Rabin asked again.

"No idea."

"Did you remember that it related in some way to Michel Hernández?"

"I guess so because on the paragraph on the little side, it has something on Michel Hernández."

"This is a letter?"

"Yes sir. A handwritten letter."

"So it is a handwritten document you are talking about?"

"Yes. And some other type documents."

"So there were two documents, a handwritten document and a typed document?"

"Yes, yes. I think it was three to four pages."

"But you didn't know how they got to you?"

"No."

"Do you know who wrote the handwritten document?"

"No."

"Did you see someone typing up a document?"

"No, not at all."

"You had never seen those documents before in your life?"

"Not at all, uh-uh."

"Was there a post mark?"

"I didn't notice any," Oquendo said after some thought.

"Did you notice if it came from the United States?"

"I guess so. All of our mail (in Puerto Rico) comes from the United States."

"No one had told you they would be sending you documents?"

"No, just I looked at it and I laughed and I called the Commissioner's office. I said there was some documents sent to me of the New York Yankees, but to be honest with you, I really don't want to discuss this because it is a letter that it would be a shame for baseball."

"So you got documents that you didn't know where they came from and you called the Commissioner's office to say that you don't know where these documents came from?"

"Absolutely."

"And you don't know what they are?"

"I know what they are because I read them."

"Do you have any individual basis for knowing that the documents you read are authentic?"

"I have no idea."

"But you still called the Commissioner's office about it?"

"Yes."

"Who did you speak to at the Commissioner's office?"

"I spoke to Lou Melendez about it."

"And what were you instructed to do?"

"Lou told me that he wanted me to send it to him and… or read it out to him, and I said, 'Lou, I really don't want to get into this because this is going to open up a can of worms. But I am just letting you know that I got this letter because you don't know who wants to harm you or what's coming. I just notified the Commissioner's office about that letter.'"

"Did you do that for your own protection? Did you notify the Commissioner's office?"

"Yes."

"Did you have any views as to somebody who would be coming to harm you?"

"I don't know."

"You thought that was a possibility when you received those documents?"

"I don't know what the intention was, but I just want to be clear on the record at this date that I did call. Thank God I did."

"Do you have a relative that works in the New York Yankees' offices in Tampa?"

"No."

"Rey Negron is not your cousin?"

"No."

This is the first Jason had ever heard the name Ray Negron. He had no idea where Rabin was going with this, and he made a note to ask Oquendo about him during the next break.

"You never asked Rey Negron to get documents for you?"

"No."

"Did you ever ask anybody else in the Yankees' Tampa office to get documents for you?"

"Why should I? After 1998 season, I wanted to start my new life with the Reds. I am very happy there. Things are great there. The past is the past."

"How did you feel when you were terminated from the Yankees?"

"Just like anybody else when you get terminated from your job, it hurts. But you have to keep on living. It happens in baseball."

"Do you know who made the decision to terminate you?"

"Mark Newman."

"Do you know if Gordon Blakeley contributed to the decision to terminate you?"

"No, not at all. He was against it."

This revealed to Jason that Oquendo had no motive against Blakeley. It was apparent he and Blakeley had a decent working relationship and in Jason's mind, Oquendo's veracity was not an issue.

Next, Rabin jumped back to when Oquendo was a Yankees' employee and questioned him about his title at the time Michel Hernández defected.

"And talk about whether you were officially given the title of Director for Scouting for Latin America?" Rabin asked.

"Gordon told me verbally and in '96 he gave it to me."

"Do you remember when in 1996 he gave it to you?"

"October. He told me that I was going to be the Latin America Coordinator."

"Okay. Do you know where it was that Gordon Blakeley said that you were going to be the Director of Scouting for Latin America?"

"He told me I was his man," Oquendo said.

"Do you recall where he told you that you were his man?"

"When you say where, what you do mean by that?"

"Where were you and where was he when this was said?"

"Together."

"Where were you together, Puerto Rico, Mexico, New York City, Tampa?"

"I couldn't tell you the place. We went all over."

"At some point, do you remember whether you were in a car, a house, outside, inside, anything about the time he told you this?"

"I do remember that he told me in the Olympics, we were in Atlanta, and he said, 'Jorge, I am going to take care of you big time.'"

"He told you at the Olympics?"

"Yes, in Atlanta."

"'Take care of you big time?'"

"And your family," Oquendo added.

"And did he say at the same time that you were going to be his Director of Scouting for Latin America?"

"Yes. He couldn't speak the language. Couldn't speak the language of Latin America, Spanish."

"And it was in the Olympic Village when he was telling you this?"

"We wasn't in the… it was only one time that I went inside the Olympic Village."

"Let's back up. I am trying to find out where it was that Gordon Blakeley told you that you were going to be his Director of Scouting for Latin America. I thought you said Atlanta. Now I am not sure whether you know it was Atlanta. Do you know where he told you that?"

"I didn't tell you he told me in Atlanta. He said he was going to take care of me in Atlanta. He told me not one time, several times."

"Take care of you?"

"Yes, and I would be his Latin American coordinator."

"What I am interested in is not if he told you he was going to take care of you. I am interested in if he told you that you were going to be his Director of Scouting for Latin America. Are you telling me that occurred more than one time?"

"Yes sir."

"Do you remember when the first time was?"

"No, I couldn't remember. He told me so many times, I forgot."

"Told you so many times you forgot?" Rabin laughed.

"Yes."

"Do you know whether he had the authority to make you Director of Scouting for Latin America?"

"I have no idea."

"Do you know who at the Yankees' organization selects the titles for people, gives titles to people?"

"I have no idea. That was Gordon Blakeley and Mr. Mark Newman at that time."

"Anybody else at the Yankees know that you were going to be Gordon Blakeley's Director of Scouting for Latin America?"

"Everybody knew I was flying all over the place."

"I want to separate that out. I understood your claim is that you flew all over the place and people knew it."

"Yes."

"But I am talking about a title here, a specific title that you were given. Did anybody know that you were the Director of Scouting for Latin America?"

"I never put that as a thought because all the scouts called me. All the Latin American scouts were calling me; Carlos Paz, Ortega, Victor Mata. All the Latin American scouts were calling me."

Jason thought to himself that this line of questioning was objectionable as having been asked and answered, but Oquendo kept answering without hesitation. He knew what he was told, and Jason was going to let Oquendo explain it as much as possible.

To Jason, Oquendo's memory was clear. He had a relationship with Blakeley and Jason was willing to let him tell his story. Jason felt that Rabin also attempted to paint Oquendo as a disgruntled former employee. They believed Oquendo was still fuming over an incident years before while he was still a Yankee. A hurricane struck Oquendo's homeland of Puerto Rico and he asked the Yankees' organization to donate money for the relief and rebuilding of the island. The Yankees promised but no help arrived. Now, the Yankees tried to portray Oquendo as resentful from being slighted by the club.

Rabin's attempt did not seem to affect Oquendo. He kept telling his story, no matter who it might involve. No one was immune. Jason felt Oquendo did a wonderful job of describing how he and Gordon Blakeley flew to Mexico to scout Hernández and handle the surrounding negotiations. But when the opportunity presented itself, Oquendo was steadfast in his attempts to testify this was not the first time the Yankees had done something like this.

Occasionally, during his testimony, Oquendo would jump into unrelated stories. For example, he told the story of the time he was asked by the Yankees to go to Cuba to scout a player. Such a story, perhaps anticipated by DuPuy, was such that DuPuy stated, and reiterated, he did not want to hear it. So with no surprise to Jason, Rabin jumped from his chair and reminded Oquendo of Bob DuPuy's instructions from the previous day. There would be no mention of Cuba or any other Cuban players, other than Hernández.

Jason felt, at that point, the message had been made clear and just to show he was calm and confident in this situation, he told Oquendo that he did not care either about other Cuban players and said, "Let's just focus on this issue."

Oquendo went so far as to discuss a time when he said the Yankees asked him to hide another player in his house in Puerto Rico. The player was a free agent, just back from playing ball in Japan. Just as Hernández, the Yankees must not have wanted any other team to have a chance to sign him.

"I should have gotten credit for that guy," Oquendo said.

"Why?" asked Rabin.

"It was all my work."

"What did you do?"

"Oh, I hid him in my house for a month and falsified his birth certificate with Mrs. Jean Afterman," Oquendo said as he glanced across the table at Mrs. Afterman.

Rabin suggested, with a seasoned lawyer's tone and timing, "Now would be a good time to take a break."

Each time the subject of Cuba or a Cuban player was brought up, Lonn Trost, the Yankee's Chief Operating Officer, would stand and walk closer to Oquendo, never averting his eyes from the witness chair. Jason assumed it was to listen closer to Oquendo's testimony, but he found it interesting this was Trost's habit each and every time Cuba was mentioned. Indeed, the testimony Oquendo offered must have been either a revelation or the first public discourse of such a sensitive, delicate subject. Steinbrenner must have wanted to be kept informed of the information revealed during the depositions, especially Oquendo's.

Jason understood Trost's actions, and without acknowledging Trost's movements or posturing, let him be. Oquendo's testimony didn't make Jason waver in the least. He never had to leave his chair during the testimony. He had a front row seat to the show.

CHAPTER 7

"Baseball is too much of a sport to be called a business, and too much of a business to be called a sport."

- Philip Wrigley

During the lunch break from the depositions, Jason and
Oquendo were escorted by Ed Burns to the "Jackie Robinson"
room down the hall where the Commissioner's office had lunch
ready for the two. Jason relished the fact that his lunch hour
would be spent in a room named after such a historical figure.
He also welcomed the break.

Oquendo, whose back was aching from sitting in an
uncomfortable chair all morning, sat on the floor and ate with
his back against the wall. Jason tried to review the morning's
testimony with Oquendo, but his curiosity was stirring about an
odd question asked by Rabin that morning. Finally, he asked
Oquendo, "Who is Ray Negron?"

"When Ray Negron was a kid, George Steinbrenner
caught him spray painting a Yankees' logo on a wall at Yankee
Stadium. Instead of punishing Negron, Steinbrenner hired him
as a bat boy. Over the years, Negron worked his way up through
the Yankees' organization and now serves as Steinbrenner's
personal assistant."

"Why did Rabin refer to Negron as your cousin?" Jason
asked.

"I have no idea. Maybe because we are both Puerto
Rican," Oquendo replied.

Oquendo said that Ray Negron was a touchy subject
within the Yankees' organization because there was apparently
some resentment of him. Oquendo believed that many in the
Yankees' front office were jealous of Negron simply because he
was treated like Steinbrenner's adopted son. Maybe someone in
the Yankees' organization was trying to "find dirt" on Negron,

and if anyone made a connection to the mysterious documents, it might spell the end of his career with the Yankees. Jason never discovered why Negron's name was thrown into the depositions because it was the last time he was mentioned.

In the afternoon session, the Yankees were still asking why Oquendo's former position with the Yankees was referred to as the Coordinator of Latin American Scouting. Jason asked for a brief recess, so he could locate and introduce into evidence a Major League Baseball Directory from 1996. Ed Burns said that he would get his from his office.

In the meantime, Jason stood in the hall waiting with Rich Rabin, who thanked Jason for being so polite when Jason let him know in advance that he planned to introduce the directory as an exhibit and not just "spring it on him." To Jason, this was standard protocol. He would expect the same courtesy from the opposing counsel, but it made him realize that such courtesies might not be the norm for the attorneys Rabin worked with on a regular basis.

Within minutes, Ed Burns returned with the baseball directory, and Jason pointed out that Oquendo's title was listed as Coordinator of Latin American Scouting. The Yankees countered with their own Media Guide that listed Oquendo as a part-time scout. The two sides argued about the title for over an hour. It was like pounding sand. Finally, Jason stated that Oquendo's title was beside the point. He reiterated that when Hernández defected, who got the phone call regarding his defection? Jorge Oquendo. This fact was undisputed. Who did Oquendo call? Gordon Blakeley. This fact was also undisputed.

Titles, however obtained, meant nothing in this particular
transaction.

By taking this route, Jason clearly demonstrated a chain
of command so that Oquendo's exact title was irrelevant. The
fact remained that if Oquendo did not have authority to scout
and sign Hernández for the Yankees, then he would not have
played such an integral part in the process.

Rabin moved back to the day the Hernández contract
was signed and the issue of dates came up again. Oquendo
verified that the contract was signed on November 3rd, 1996 but
was dated November 21st. During this discussion, Rabin asked
the ridiculous question, "How is it that you know that you were
not in Yucatan on November 21, 1996?" It's not clear whether
this was a back-handed comment directed at Oquendo, but
Oquendo knew where he was on November 21, 1996 and it was
not in Mexico.

There were two times that afternoon where Rabin and
Oquendo became frustrated by their differences in semantics.
The first concerned the time of night when Ricalde arrived at
the hotel in Yucatan with the contract for Oquendo to sign.

"I thought you said before that when Ricalde showed up
with the notary it was the middle of the night," Rabin asked.

"When you say middle of the night, what do you mean
by middle of the night? Twelve at night?"

"Yes."

"Oh, my bad then. I misunderstood you."

The second miscommunication surrounded the term
"signed a player," which Rabin understood to mean that

Oquendo literally signed the contract of a player. Oquendo meant that he did the leg work to get a player to sign. Whether or not he actually signed the contract was of no concern to Oquendo.

Next Rabin inquired about the actual process of scouting a player and the methods used to determine a player's value, specifically Cuban players in 1996.

Rabin asked, "So if you had Player A and Player B, in those days, and one was Cuban and one was Mexican and they were of exactly equal talent, you think it would cost more to sign the Cuban in that day?"

Oquendo responded, "At that time, yes. The market for Cuban players was higher at that time."

Rabin then asked, "So the Yankees bought into that philosophy in 1996?"

"[The Yankees] spent more than that. That's peanuts."

Rabin began a different line of questioning regarding what the Yankees paid for Hernández and what happened after the contract was signed. Oquendo said that after the deal was reached for Hernández, "Gordon Blakeley hugged me, 'Jorge - five hundred thousand dollars - that's a bargain deal. Go get it done because in three or four years, we don't know where we are going to be. So let's take the player, get it done, and from then on, we take over.' That's what we did."

"That's a bargain deal, to sign the player at five hundred thousand dollars right now?" Rabin asked.

"Yeah, because we didn't have to pay a penny for the player."

"Now, if the player eventually was going to play for the Yankees, he would have to sign with the Yankees, right?"

"Yes sir."

"And the Yankees would have to pay to sign the player?"

"Yes sir."

"So they would have to pay money before he got to be in the Yankee organization?"

"Yeah, but the Yankees demand the money that was going to be given to him."

"The Yankees what?" Rabin asked.

"The Yankees, after that point, the Yankees would determine what kind of money he was going to get."

"I don't see that in this agreement anywhere."

"Because this agreement was done with Ricalde. We got another agreement," Oquendo said.

"You are saying that you have another agreement other than this agreement?"

"Yes sir."

"With the player directly?"

"Not me, Gordon Blakeley."

"At the same time [as this agreement]?"

"Yes sir."

"You have seen this agreement?"

"It was done by [Gordon Blakeley] and Gus Dominguez."

"Is it a written agreement?"

"Ask Gordon," Oquendo said.

"And you have personal knowledge of this?"

"Absolutely. Gus Dominguez' right-hand man flew into Mexico with Kenny Dominguez and they flew [Hernández] into Mexico City, and from Mexico City, they flew him into Venezuela because we couldn't do all the dirty work. So Gordon called an agent to do the dirty work. Gordon called Gus Dominguez and said, 'We are going to give this guy fifty, sixty, seventy thousand dollars, will you do the job? We will pay the expenses.'"

"What is your basis for saying that?" Rabin questioned.

"It is a fact."

"I am not interested in facts unless you heard them. Did you hear that conversation?"

"Yes, Gordon told me."

"Gordon told that to you?"

"Yes."

"When?"

"Up in the room."

"At the Yucatan Lions' facility?"

"Yes, he said, 'I am going to call my buddy Gus Dominguez; he is going to take over from here.'"

"Did he say anything other than, 'I am going to call my buddy, Gus Dominguez; he is going to take over from here?' Is that what Gordon said?"

"Yes, and I told him, 'Now it is going to cost a lot of money because now we got an agent involved.' He said, 'Jorge, don't worry about it. This is our player. We will tell Gus what the player is worth.' I said, 'Okay, bye-bye.'"

"Is that the extent of the conversations you had with Gordon Blakeley on that subject?"

"Yes sir."

"Did you ever see any document in writing regarding anything to do with this player?"

"No sir. But at the end, he came in and got the player," Oquendo said, referring to Gus Dominguez.

"At the end, do you mean 1998?"

"No, no, sir. After I did this contract. I signed it, I spent one more day because of a tournament in Puerto Rico and I had to wait for Kenny Dominguez to fly in because Kenny Dominguez spoke both languages. That day, me and Gordon went with Michel Hernández. Gordon, with his personal credit card, bought Michel Hernández a lot of clothes."

"Okay."

"Then we came back to the hotel. I flew out the next day. The next day, Kenny Dominguez came in with a gentleman that worked for Gus Dominguez and they falsified the documents, they made [Hernández] a Mexican and flew him out of the country."

"Who is they, who is they? First of all, do you have any basis for the knowledge? Did you see someone falsifying documents? Were you witnessing anybody falsifying documents?"

"[It was] the only way you could get him out."

"I am not interested in your extrapolations or hypotheses," Rabin snapped.

"[I know] because they told me."

"Who told you?"

"Kenny Dominguez."

"That he falsified documents?"

"Yes, and Gus Dominguez told me that when I spoke to him."

"Did Gus or Kenny?"

"Both, both. They flew him from Yucatan to Mexico City and I spoke to them."

"When was it that Kenny Dominguez told you that he personally falsified documents?"

"Not Kenny. It is two different persons with the last name the same."

"Gus Dominguez?"

"Yes."

"Do you have any evidence that anybody with the Yankees falsified documents?"

"No, that's why we called the agent to do the dirty job."

"You testified as to exactly what Gordon Blakeley told you when you called in Gus Dominguez?"

"Yes."

"When you say to do the dirty job, is there anything else you are referring to other than the previous conversation you mentioned with Gordon Blakeley calling Gus Dominguez?"

"I go up the room. He says, 'Jorge, I just got off the phone with Gus Dominguez. His right-hand man is going to fly to Yucatan tomorrow. They are going to prepare his paperwork. They are going to fly him from Yucatan to Mexico City. His papers are going to get done in Mexico City as a Cuban --

excuse me, as a Mexican person so he can get inside Venezuela.' Once they did that, Raul Ortega, our scout in Venezuela, picked him up."

"Which of this stuff is Gordon telling you or not?"

"He told me he was going to get Gus Dominguez to do the dirty work."

"Did he use the words 'dirty work?'"

"Absolutely, 'dirty work.'"

"We keep going over the same ground and the story keeps changing and I want to get it right. The second time it was a far more limited version of events that Gordon was telling you. Now he is using the words 'dirty work.' What is the truth, what did he tell you in that room regarding Michel Hernández?" Rabin asked.

"I just got off the phone with Gus Dominguez and he is going to do the dirty work or whatever work was done."

"Did he use the words 'dirty work' or not? Can you verify under oath today that he used the words, 'dirty work'?"

"I think he used that. 'We don't want to get involved with that, Jorge, once Gus Dominguez will clear him as a free agent, we will sign him.' That was it."

After shuffling through some of his notes, Rabin asked Oquendo about Hernández' situation once he was in Venezuela. Oquendo reiterated that Raul Ortega, the Yankees' scout in Venezuela, picked up Hernández from the airport upon his arrival and delivered him to the family home of Gus Dominguez' partner, where Hernández was to live. Before Dominguez flew him out of Mexico, Hernández had given

Oquendo his mother's phone number in Cuba. He asked
Oquendo to call her to let her know what was going on and that
he was okay. After this last question, Rabin concluded his
direct examination of Oquendo and passed the witness.

The group paused for a few moments while Jason
prepared his notes for the cross examination. Then Jason began.
He asked Oquendo, "Over that two-year period of time (that
Hernández lived in Venezuela), did you maintain contact with
his (Hernández') mother?"

Oquendo said, "I always used to give her a call. Always
'Michel is doing okay' because they never allowed Michel to
use the phone."

"Who wouldn't allow Michel to use the phone?" Jason
asked.

"Gus Dominguez didn't want him to or Gordon
(Blakeley)."

"Why?" Jason asked.

"Ask them."

"How do you know?"

"Because Michel told me."

"Are there logs or records that would show your phone
calls?" Jason asked.

"When I send my telephone expenses, the phone calls to
Cuba and Michel, by Gordon's orders, he says put a magic
marker over that and make a photo copy of that and send it in,
so nobody could trace our calls."

Oquendo went on to explain that after several months of
paying Michel Hernández' expenses, Gus Dominguez, the agent

who helped get Hernández out of Mexico, was fed up. From that point, all expenses related to Hernández were to be paid as if they were an expense for the local Yankees' scout, Raul Ortega. According to Oquendo, this action was directly approved by Gordon Blakeley.

Next Jason produced the letter Gordon Blakeley wrote to Oquendo commending him on a job well done in signing two players from Nicaragua. Jason asserted that for Blakeley to write such a letter proved that Oquendo was not simply a scout. Jason believed this letter showed the relationship between Oquendo and Blakeley and that Oquendo was not merely an "underling" but a man with authority within the Yankees' organization.

Early that evening, during Jason's cross examination, everyone present at the deposition was becoming tired and irritable. This fact and several questions regarding Cuba and Cuban players caused the testimony and the attorneys to become heated.

"You testified earlier that things were getting hot with regard to Cuban players around 1996. Do you recall that?" Jason asked Oquendo.

"I will object to the extent that you are getting into anything other than Michel Hernández," Rabin injected.

"Did you ever work with Gustavo subsequent to the Michel Hernández deal regarding Cuban players?" Jason asked.

"If you are going to get into issues relating to Cuban players other than Michel Hernández or allegations, I am not going to sit here for it. If you want to get into things other than Michel Hernández, we will get Bob DuPuy or anyone else to sit in on that. This is an alleged contract case involving a particular player. If you want to focus on that, that's fine, you can ask all the questions you want. I think Bob has been clear about that, too, by the way," Rabin said heatedly.

"Were you ever given authority to meet other Cuban players such as you did with Michel Hernández?" Jason asked Oquendo.

Rabin again jumped in, "Objection. If you are going to go into this question, let's get Bob or whoever it is, Ed, that you report to up in a contract action involving a particular player in 1996. I don't think he will have too much trouble ruling on that. If you want it do it, that's how we will do it. We will not sneak in testimony on something that you are trying to get in obviously that has nothing to do with anything. So tell me what you want to do."

"You opened the door involving any other involvements that he had with Gus (Dominguez) subsequent to the deal with Hernández," Jason said.

"I was trying to find out his relationship with Gus," Rabin responded.

"I think he testified that there may have been other issues regarding Cuban players."

"I don't know what you want me to tell you. If you want to do… get in this, get Bob DuPuy down here and we will argue it in front of him."

"We will move on," Jason conceded because he understood DuPuy's directive and he believed that his argument the Yankees opened the door to those discussions would be overruled.

Jason attempted to work around the mention of Cuba when he asked Oquendo, "What countries, per Gordon Blakeley's authority, did you go to, to scout a player?"

Rabin injected, "Provided that you will not mention Cuba."

Oquendo said to Rabin, "You mentioned it for me!"

Rabin took on an angrier tone when he responded, "I'm just trying to make sure that you're not trying to fish to get something that has nothing to do with this case. It's six o'clock in the night and it just seems to me that you've got some separate agenda other than this case, and frankly we've seen enough today. If you want to ask him these questions, if I'm wrong about where you're going with it or what you're trying to do, I apologize, but I want to make it clear to you and I want it clear to the witness that we're staying on this case right now."

Jason responded, "That's fine and I don't need to hear Cuba. I don't know if this individual has ever been to Cuba. I don't care if he's ever been to Cuba. But, the point is, I want him to list me what countries he's been to as Coordinator of Latin America Scouting."

Rabin said, "Okay, as long as we understand each other, absolutely." Jason felt that Rabin inadvertently accepted Jason's referral to Oquendo as the Coordinator of Latin America Scouting.

Rabin continued, "You asked a couple of questions and he seemed to be trying to get into it and I friggin' don't know what he's going to say. I just want to stay on the path here."

Jason turned his attention back to Oquendo and asked, "Other than Cuba, where have you been?"

Oquendo turned to Rabin and answered, "Whether you like it, or not, I'm gonna say it. If I was sent into Cuba, I'm going to say it."

Rabin said heatedly, "You will not get into that."

Jason, trying to calm everyone down, said, "Let's move on, my direct question is: Other than Cuba…"

Oquendo interrupted, "If I was…"

"Listen, Mr. Oquendo," Rabin interrupted, "I'm going to demand that you not get in to this right now!"

"Okay," Oquendo replied.

Rabin continued, "You're not being asked a question about whether you went to Cuba."

"Okay," again Oquendo replied.

"Mr. Browning has been clear about that," Rabin added.

"Okay," Oquendo said.

"You're being asked about whether you'd been to other countries," Rabin stated.

Oquendo turned back to Jason, "Let's follow on. Let's go Jason."

"My specific question, what countries, other than Cuba, I don't want to hear Cuba, have you visited as Coordinator of Latin American Scouting?" Jason asked.

"But I been to Cuba!" Oquendo blurted.

"Not…" was all Jason could get out before Rabin interrupted.

"I move to strike it and, frankly, if it happens again, I'm going to end the depositions for today," Rabin said, then turned to Oquendo and continued, "You're not here to offer pontification."

"Okay," Oquendo said.

Jason again asked Oquendo, "List for me other countries."

"I'm just warning you Jason, the tape's about over." Rabin said.

"That's fine; change it."

By the time tape four was set up to record, it was approaching seven o'clock in the evening and Jason was ready to get to the end of Oquendo's deposition. Rabin began by asking Oquendo general Yankees' scouting questions.

"Who was the most important scout in the Yankees' organization in 1996?"

"Excuse me, say that again," Oquendo replied.

"Was Gene Michael kind of the Yankees' super scout in 1996?"

Oquendo grinned as he answered, "Nobody's a super scout for the Yankees. Whoever's the hot man that kisses George (Steinbrenner), that's the hot scout."

Rabin then asked about the role George Steinbrenner's son-in-law played in the Yankees' organization.

Oquendo replied, "He ran everything down there. When he divorced Steinbrenner's daughter, Steinbrenner fired him."

The duration of the deposition continued with relatively meaningless questions from the Yankee's counsel. Just before the deposition was concluded, Oquendo asked, "Can I say something?"

"No!" Both Jason and Rabin replied.

Oquendo smiled at the response. Jason knew Oquendo was willing to say just about anything that crossed his mind. Oquendo had done his job. Jason felt his testimony, despite the occasional outburst, ultimately made their case and on a grander scale, revealed the apparent inner workings of the international baseball market.

Oquendo's testimony made Jason realize why he ultimately took on this case. What surprised him was the role cultural differences played in its unfolding. Oquendo and Ricalde were not after wealth or notoriety; they simply wished to right a wrong. The petty arguments presented by the American attorneys made little difference to them. The simple fact was that someone promised they were going to abide by an agreement, and they didn't. Points were made regarding the misdating of the contract, along with many other attempts at character assassination, but the bottom line was that, in certain parts of the world, a simple handshake was enough to be considered binding.

Jason thought it was odd that Ed Burns, who sat next to him taking notes the entire day, never showed any reaction or emotion during Oquendo's testimony. Jason wondered if any of the day's revelations were a surprise to Burns. Did Major League Baseball already know of what transpired in the international baseball market, or did they simply give Jason an open path to see where the young attorney might lead? Or, were they providing the rope for Jason to hang himself?

After the depositions wrapped up, Jason and Oquendo returned to their hotel to have dinner. While eating, Oquendo constantly asked Jason how he performed during his deposition. Oquendo was fascinated by the process and Jason felt he took great pride in being part of the procedure. Jason reassured Oquendo that he did well and that he was satisfied with the outcome so far.

After a casual debriefing, Jason turned his attention to the final day of the depositions. He had to prepare for perhaps the most important witness, Gordon Blakeley. Sleep was hard to come by for Jason on Thursday night. He was worried that Blakeley might simply walk into the depositions and deny everything. The entire case was based upon the testimony of Ricalde and Oquendo, which was strong but only represented one side of the story. He knew they had hotel and flight receipts proving Blakeley was in Mexico on the dates in question, but what if Blakeley claimed he was in Mexico to scout another player? Different scenarios played through Jason's head all night. The few hours he did manage to sleep were anything but restful.

CHAPTER 8

"Good pitching will always stop good hitting and vice-versa."
- Casey Stengel

Friday morning Gordon Blakeley appeared relaxed for his deposition. Unlike Oquendo, Blakeley was not rocking in his chair or doing anything to appear uncomfortable. He was a well-built man who appeared to be in his late-40's, with graying hair and an intense stare. To exemplify Blakeley's apparent confidence, his neatly pressed white dress shirt showed no wrinkles or signs of wear.

Jason planned to begin his questioning of Blakeley with general, non-threatening conversation about his experience and his current employment with the Yankees. He would get Blakeley relaxed and then hit him with what he hoped would be calculated, well-placed strikes. This was always Jason's way to get the information he needed. The New York attorneys might badger a witness until they got their answer, but Jason had had better luck when he took a subdued approach. Jason did not worry about the overall mood of the other participants that day. He concentrated on Blakeley's testimony. It could either reinforce his client's case or render it impotent. He knew he would have an answer within the day.

Jason made his official introduction for the record and said, "I am from Fort Smith, Arkansas. Please don't laugh." The statement was an appreciated joke in the room, but it was also a reminder that he was the perceived underdog going up against a world-renowned organization.

Jason began by peering into Blakeley's background. Gordon Alexander Blakeley attended Chapman University in California, where he played baseball. Before graduation, Blakeley was drafted by the Detroit Tigers in the nineteenth round as a third baseman. In 1978 he was released by the Tigers and returned to Chapman to finish his undergraduate degree, followed by a Master's degree from Cal-Poly in Secondary Education. Blakeley coached high school baseball and taught physical education for several years before being hired as a scout for the Seattle Mariners in 1989.

In 1990, Blakeley was promoted to East Coast Supervising Scout for the Mariners and he was moved to Tampa, Florida. In 1994, Blakeley was hired away by the New York Yankees to serve as Scouting Coordinator for the Pacific Rim. In 1995, he was promoted to Director of International Scouting for the Yankees, a title that Blakeley admitted was very similar to Coordinator. Just as Oquendo had done, Blakeley regarded titles with the Yankees as a secondary concern. He simply knew his job entailed scouting the Latin American baseball market.

Jason asked Blakeley to look at the Yankees' Media Guide from 1996 and asked, "Are you familiar with the scouts listed here?"

Blakeley honed in on two Canadians listed as foreign scouts and said, "These scouts were not truly foreign scouts because Canada participates in the amateur draft." This demonstrated that the Yankees' Media Guide was, in fact, not infallible, and just as Oquendo stated, could contain mistakes related to personnel titles. When asked by Jason, Blakeley admitted the guide provided by Rabin could contain mistakes.

Jason then asked questions about Oquendo's responsibilities within the Yankees' organization.

Blakeley said, "Oquendo's main responsibility was scouting within Puerto Rico."

Jason asked, "What do you mean by 'main responsibility'?"

"Just because a scout has one area of responsibility, he may be asked to do other things or go other places."

"Could you be more specific?" Jason asked.

Blakeley said, "Oquendo was asked to go to countries that were less productive when it came to finding Major League Baseball level talent."

"Why was Mr. Oquendo asked to go into these countries?"

"Because Oquendo was a citizen of Puerto Rico, so he had an American passport, which made it much easier for him to move about the Latin American countries than many of the other scouts."

"Okay, when it comes to signing a player and the term 'signed' is used, could you explain what that term means?"

"The term 'signed' for a player doesn't necessarily mean the scout actually signed the contract. The scout may have simply done the majority of the leg work to get the player signed with the team." Blakeley said.

Jason then asked Blakeley if he was familiar with Señor Gustavo Ricalde.

"No, I'm not," Blakeley answered. "It doesn't ring a bell."

"Does that mean you've never met him?" Jason asked.

"It means I don't recall. I don't recall that name."

"In 1996, did you know who the owner of the Yucatan Lions was?"

Rabin injected, "Could you clarify when in 1996. I'm going to object to the question."

Jason continued, "May 31, 1996, did you know who the owner of the Yucatan Lions was?"

"I don't think I did. I don't recall that I did."

Jason found it interesting that Blakeley did not recall the name of the owner of a club the Yankees had a working agreement with in 1996, but this was just the beginning of Blakeley's fuzzy memory.

Blakeley confirmed that Oquendo first notified him of Hernández' defection but more importantly, he confirmed that he discussed this with Mark Newman and Newman told Blakeley to go down to Mexico and evaluate Hernández.

Jason questioned Blakeley about the events surrounding his trip to Mexico to first meet Hernández. Blakeley had trouble recalling if it was actually Oquendo who first called him regarding Hernández defection. Then he didn't recall whether or not he and Oquendo met in Miami and then flew to Mexico or if they flew separately.

And when Jason asked who picked him up from the airport in Mexico, Blakeley said, "To the best of my recollection, somebody picked us up." Blakeley could not remember if he flew with Oquendo, but in the next statement he made, he said someone picked *us* up from the airport although Oquendo was already in Mexico when Blakeley arrived.

It doesn't take long for an attorney who receives answers like this to understand that his work may be cut out for him. Blakeley was somebody Jason would have to, throughout the questioning, follow up with due to the vague, sometime elusive answers. Perhaps Blakeley's vast experience in scouting had clouded his memory. His unclear, and oftentimes complete lapses in memory, made Jason question his veracity altogether. The only thing to do with witnesses like this was to press forward.

This would be the beginning of countless "I don't recall" or "I don't remember" answers from Blakeley. Once he said, "You're asking me to remember, eight years ago, what I did when I got to the hotel? I don't remember."

All of the other witnesses during the depositions remembered a great deal about that fateful night in Mexico, but Blakeley, an executive with the New York Yankees, could not. Some details he recalled immediately. For example, when he was asked whether Hernández was right-handed or left-handed, he immediately answered "right-handed."

Blakeley said he went to the Lions' stadium to watch Hernández practice with the Yucatan team. He believed the practice took place at night because he specifically recalled the stadium lights were on. When asked about the players present, he stated that there were approximately fifteen to twenty-five players there, all in uniform with the exception of Hernández. Blakeley did not term this activity a workout. He said, typically, that during a workout, the player(s) would run a sixty-yard dash and this was not the case with Hernández. It was simply a practice observed, according to Blakeley. Jason filed this response away in his mind. "A practice with the Yucatan team in November? Impossible," Jason thought.

Jason next inquired about Blakeley's thoughts on Hernández' physical abilities. Blakeley read through the scouting report and agreed with its conclusions with the exception of the term 'quick bat.' He did not agree with that statement.

Blakeley said, "Catch and throw were his best tools."

"How was his arm?" Jason asked.

"He threw well."

Jason handed Blakeley an exhibit that contained a scouting report and asked, "Could you tell me the date of the report and who filled it out?"

The report stated that it was filled out by Oquendo but Blakeley said, "Just because a scouting report has a date on it, it doesn't mean that's when the report was generated. If this was Oquendo's report, and by the way, a scout could go in and anybody could put a name in and submit the report under someone else's name at this particular time. According to this report here, or whoever typed in Oquendo, they saw him play a game on 11/3/96."

"Is it your testimony that this may not have been filled out by Mr. Oquendo?" Jason asked.

Rabin injected, "I believe his testimony is clear that he doesn't know who filled it out but that Oquendo's name is on the form."

Jason thought that it was amazing that, even in 1996, the Yankees' scouting endeavors relied on a reporting system that could so easily be manipulated to produce scouting reports with potentially false dates and/or false submitters.

Jason asked Blakeley to read the summary at the bottom of the report on Hernández. Among several other items, it said that Hernández "doesn't want to go back to Cuba," which Blakeley said was obvious.

"Why is that obvious?" Jason asked.

"Because he'd go to prison," Blakeley answered.

Jason then took Blakeley back to the visit to Mexico and asked what Blakeley did when he arrived back at the hotel after watching Hernández practice. Blakeley said that he was sure that he must have called Mark Newman, his boss.

"When you called Mark Newman, would you have discussed Hernández?" Jason asked.

"Sure," Blakeley said.

"What would you have discussed?"

"I'd say there's a Cuban player, a catcher, that I just saw in practice and he's a defector and we would discuss what needs to be done or where do we go from here," Blakeley said.

"And what needed to be done?" Jason asked.

"We couldn't do anything. One of two things had to happen: he either had to come into the States with a representative and go through the draft, or he had to go to a country, establish residency and become a free agent."

"And what did you decide?"

"We decided to call an agent and let them handle this," Blakeley said.

"What agent?" Jason asked.

"My recollection, we called two agents: Joe Cubas and Gus Dominguez. I don't remember if I called them, Mark (Newman) called them or he called one and I called the other, but one of us spoke to Gus Dominguez. We called both. We got in touch with Gus first."

"Why did you contact these two?"

"They're both Cuban agents, both of them have had Cuban clients and at that time, to the best of my recollection, they were the only two who were dealing with Cuban defectors."

Jason was familiar with both agents Blakeley had named but he questioned whether Cubas was actually contacted. This was a point Jason made sure to remember because, as the way the transaction came to fruition, it was very important to know who indeed played a role in this endeavor. This didn't even address the fact that Jason was learning, through Blakeley himself, that Blakeley was a major participant in getting Michel out of Mexico.

Ironically, as nondescript as his testimony was, Blakeley revealed plenty. There was no doubt in Jason's mind now that Blakeley had played a major role in this transaction from the moment he boarded the plane bound for Yucatan.

In Cubas' Affidavit of Fact that Jason had obtained following the depositions, Cubas stated: *"...it is my understanding that, at some point during this process, through briefs and/or depositions, Mr. Blakeley has claimed that he called me, as well as Mr. Dominguez to inform me of Mr. Hernández' defection. Let it be known that I did not receive any*

phone calls from Mr. Blakeley, Mr. Oquendo or any other
Yankee personnel to inform me of Mr. Hernández' defection or
availability."

Cubas went further to explain why he would not have
been contacted by Blakeley. He alleges: *"...due to my differences*
with Mr. Blakeley originating specifically during a meeting in
January of 1996 at the Plaza Naco Hotel in the Dominican
Republic...Mr. Blakeley attempted to bribe me with a 'payoff' if
I delivered to the Yankees then client and also Cuban Defector,
Mr. Livan Hernández. As a result of my immediate angered
response, refusal and adverse reaction to Mr. Blakeley's
proposal, since then, the Yankees and/or Mr. Blakeley have
refrained from having Mr. Blakeley participate directly in any
discussions and/or any negotiations for players represented by
my firm..."

In another section of Cubas' statement, he referred to the
Yankees actions as *"an effort to conceal Mr. Hernández*
[Michel] from other Major League Clubs and other player
agents..."

Cubas believed the Yankees' representatives and the
agent, Gus Dominguez, took advantage of Hernández' lack of
knowledge regarding the signing process: *"As a result, due to*
Mr. Hernández' lack of knowledge specifically, on Major
League Rules, The Commissioner's office "unblocking" process
to scout and sign Cuban Nationals, related immigration issues
and the fear of being sent back to Cuba to face incarceration,
Mr. Hernández agreed to sign a contract with the Yankees in
the amount of $60,000."

Blakeley said he did not give Oquendo permission to negotiate for Hernández and that Oquendo did not show him the contract now in question. The only terms he recalled negotiating had to do with the working agreement between the Lions and Yankees. Blakeley said that Mark Newman had told him that he might have to deal with some working agreement issues while in Mexico. He did not recall what he did the day after the contract was signed in Merida, but he said that he "obviously had to eat." Blakeley did recall buying clothes for Hernández. To most, this would have the appearance of a good-hearted gesture, and no doubt may have been, but with Michel still being a Cuban resident, not unblocked by Major League rules, it was this type of innocent activity that revealed the Yankees' premier position in signing the soon-to-be free agent.

Hernández was signed to a minor league contract with the Yankees on May 11, 1998, nearly a year and a half after he defected from Cuba.

Jason asked Blakeley, "Did you participate in the negotiation of this contract with Gus Dominguez?"

"Yes. Hernández received a sixty-thousand dollar signing bonus."

Jason showed Blakeley a copy of Hernández' contract and asked, "Are these your handwritten notes on the addendum?"

"I don't know," Blakeley responded.

"Did the Yankees help to pay Hernández' expenses while he lived in Venezuela?"

"Only after he had signed with the Yankees," Blakeley said.

Jason asked, "Did you have any discussions regarding a signing bonus for Hernández before he actually signed with the Yankees?"

"No."

Jason had no more questions for Blakeley. When Rabin began his cross examination, he questioned Blakeley again about the way the Yankees assigned titles.

Blakeley said, "Sometimes the Yankees gave an employee a better title to keep them from jumping ship." Though not necessarily a promotion, a new title would many times appease an employee and deter them from leaving for another organization. In most instances, the new title did not come with a raise in salary.

Rabin pulled out the Yankees Media Guide from 1996 and asked Blakeley several questions about Yankees' scouts in various regions. It was interesting that Blakeley corrected Rabin's pronunciation of a Canadian scout's name but then said he was "not familiar with the scout."

During the period when Hernández was living in Venezuela, Blakeley admitted making frequent calls to Gus Dominguez to inquire about the status of Hernández's citizenship. Blakeley knew Hernández must establish his citizenship in Venezuela before he could enter America. This could take as long as two years.

Jason asked Blakeley, "If you understood the free agency rules of Major League Baseball and Hernández were to become a Venezuelan resident therefore he would become "unblocked" and would be able to sign with any Major League team as a free agent, why, over the span of two years did you constantly call to check on Hernández? Why would you care?"

Blakeley said it was simply because he was interested in Hernández. That interest, as Jason always believed, was a vested interest in Hernández. As Jason understood, and no evidence has since proven otherwise, the Yankees had already signed Hernández "under the table" and had invested thousands of dollars in securing his signing while he was housed in Venezuela. They were keeping tabs on their "property." Blakeley did not sign the contract to purchase the rights to Hernández from the Yucatan Lions, so it was easy for him to claim no knowledge of the agreement. But, as was asked before, why would Ricalde allow Blakeley to arrange Hernández' trip out of Mexico if there had been no contract in place?

If the Yankees had no agreement in place with Hernández, he could have played baseball in Venezuela while awaiting his citizenship. Once his citizenship was established, a memo would have been sent to every Major League Baseball team notifying them of Hernández' unblocked status. He would have been unblocked because he would no longer have been a Cuban citizen. At that point, any team could have negotiated with Hernández or his agent. That was not how it happened.

On January 7, 1998, the Commissioner's office sent to all Major League teams a memo that was simply titled 'Cuban player available.' In the memo it was revealed that, *"Mr. Hernández was a traveling member of the Cuban National*

Juvenile team when he defected while in Colombia in October 1996."

Such a memo made it apparent to Jason that the Commissioner's office, which confirms that a player has been "unblocked," was not provided accurate or complete information on Michel's defection. How they came up with this information perplexed Jason. However, he never had a doubt that the memo was wholly inaccurate. Gordon Blakeley's testimony alone explained the workings of Michel's travels, and Colombia was never a part of the itinerary. Obviously, at that time, Gus Dominguez still served as Hernández' gatekeeper. In a gesture to give credence to the free agent market, the memo states at the end, *"I have informed his representative, Mr. Dominguez that all clubs are to refrain from negotiating terms until Monday, January 12, 1998 to allow everyone enough time to retrieve this memo. At which time, information will be sent to you by Mr. Dominguez regarding his client."*

Jason continued his questioning of Blakeley, "Any particular reason the Yankees would have helped Michel Hernández get to Venezuela, if he was going to be subject to free agency?"

Rabin jumped in, "Objection. You characterized that the Yankees helped him get to Venezuela. That has not been the testimony. So I am going to instruct you not to answer that question. You mischaracterized the testimony."

"It is your testimony that you and/or Mr. Newman contacted, spoke with at some point in time Gus Dominguez in regard to Michel Hernández, correct?" Jason asked.

"One of us talked to Gus Dominguez?" Blakeley asked.

"Yes," Jason said.

"In regards to Michel Hernández?" Blakeley asked.

"Yes," Jason said.

"Yes," Blakeley answered.

"And Kenny Dominguez, an employee of the Yankees, either flew to Merida or Mexico City to meet with Michel Hernández?"

"I don't know necessarily he flew there to meet…"

"I think you… maybe not 'meet', but I think the term you used was 'hand off,' and if the Yankees were to hand off Michel Hernández to Gus Dominguez or a representative of Gus Dominguez, why would they have done that if the Yankees knew he was going to have to be a free agent?"

"He wasn't necessarily going to have to be a free agent."

"What was he going to have to be before the Yankees could sign him?" Jason asked.

"He had two options; they made a decision to go to a third country and establish residency. If he went to the U.S., he would have to participate in the draft. They made that decision."

"'They' being who?"

"Gus Dominguez and the player."

Jason considered such a response by Blakeley to be irrational. He was hard-pressed to accept the fact that Michel Hernández had the option of becoming subject to the draft because the Yankees would never have sent anybody, including Oquendo, to Yucatan to scout Hernández if he were to choose to become a U.S. citizen, therefore subject to the amateur draft.

With this, it was not in a Cuban player's, much less his agent's, best interest to subject the player to the draft when an open market was available. There was little chance Hernández was going to become a U.S. citizen.

It was now Rabin's turn for cross examination, and he questioned Blakeley about several players recommended by Jorge Oquendo during his career with the Yankees.

"Could I have you look at Exhibit 14?" Rabin asked.

"Yeah."

"The contract for Thiago Kussano; did this guy make it big in your recollection?"

"No," Blakeley answered.

"What do you remember about this gentleman?"

"He was a bad sign."

"A bad sign. Do you remember how much money he was signed for, approximately?"

"Roughly $25,000."

"And you don't think he ever made the big leagues?"

"He never got out of the Dominican League."

"This was not a good recommendation by Jorge Oquendo?" Rabin asked.

"I didn't think it was a good recommendation."

"Do you remember the name Felix Rodriguez? That is the next one, number 15."

"No. I said before I don't remember. I don't remember."

"How many players are in the organization now that were signed through the foreign scouts, if you had to estimate?"

"It is well over 100."

"So there are a lot of players being signed every year, fair to say?"

"I would say we sign between 25 and 35," Blakeley said.

"I take it you don't remember every one of their names?"

"I remember their names as they are signed, because I would have talked to the scout about the recommendation. But then I may not remember them now."

"Sitting here today, do you have reason to believe that Felix Rodriguez was an excellent sign?"

"I would say no. He would not be."

"Why would you say that?"

"Because he too, apparently, never got out of the Dominican, because if he got to Tampa on Gulf Coast League, I would have remembered him."

"Alexander Mora, do you remember how much he was signed for?"

"I would say roughly in the five to fifteen thousand dollar range."

"Do you remember what became of him?"

"He never… I don't believe he ever made it to Tampa, to the Gulf Coast League."

"What about Cristian Enrique Mendosa Castellon?"

"As far as how much he signed for?"

"Yes."

"Again, I think he was a five to fifteen thousand dollar sign, somewhere in that ballpark."

"Do you remember what happened to him?"

"He pitched in the Dominican two summers, and then he pitched in the Gulf Coast League. He never got out of A Ball. He was a release."

Blakeley recalled many details about most of the players about which Rabin asked. Most curiously, Blakeley seemed to remember the amount of the signing bonus for each of the players. Even questions requiring some degree of speculation, Blakeley answered for Rabin with no hesitation. In thirty minutes of cross examination by Rabin, Blakeley only answered "I don't recall" or "I don't remember" three times, whereas for Jason, it was a regular occurrence.

"Was Jorge Oquendo terminated from the New York Yankee organization?" Rabin asked.

"He was not rehired," Blakeley said.

"Sitting here today, do you know the reasons why?"

"We did not renew his contract. He had a difficult time figuring out [an average] OFP versus [a good] OFP (Overall Future Potential). He had a tough time determining if a player is worth ten thousand dollars or a million dollars. There were some expense issues that we were not happy with."

"Can you explain that?"

"For his job situation, he ran high expenses in comparison to other scouts."

"Other area scouts?"

"Yes."

Jason had a chance to respond, "Mr. Blakeley, you testified that Oquendo had difficulty or a difficult time figuring out [an average] OFP versus [a good] OFP?" Jason asked.

"That's correct."

"When did you discover that Mr. Oquendo was having difficulty making that distinction?"

"I don't know if it was a specific date or year. I don't remember when we terminated him or did not renew his contract, but it was over a period of time. His reports, his being able to slot players and put a value on them had not improved."

"Did you ever have any discussions with Oquendo about his evaluation?"

"I don't recall, but I'm sure, because we used to discuss players, I would have said, 'I think you are high on this player, too low on this player.'"

"Do the Yankees have a scale to equate dollar value to a certain OFP?"

"Yeah, I believe we do."

"Was Oquendo provided this scale?"

"Yes."

"He was?" Jason asked again.

"I'm sure he was. He attended scouting meetings."

"Were all scouts provided this scale?"

"All scouts that attended… we had scouting meetings in January that were run by our scouting director. And there would be frequent discussion about matching [a players potential] with dollars and draft, where they would fit in the draft."

Jason wanted to show that if the Yankees provided a scale to determine a player's value, how could Oquendo even get that far off in his player value determinations? He certainly could not arbitrarily, on his own, determine what the Yankees should pay for a player.

Blakeley's deposition was concluded at 4:30 that afternoon. Jason was relieved to find that Blakeley freely admitted to what he believed were the important issues of the case. He admitted that he was in Mexico in November of 1996 to scout Michel Hernández (or to watch him workout with the Yucatan team), whom Blakeley admitted was a Cuban defector and therefore out of reach of teams within Major League Baseball.

The points he did not admit to he simply responded by saying "I don't remember" or "I don't recall." Jason was also pleased that Blakeley admitted that Gus Dominguez was involved in the "hand off" of Hernández. At one point, he found himself thinking, "This guy is admitting to a lot of shit!" His testimony made the introduction of the mystery documents unnecessary. Blakeley's testimony was all Jason needed. Besides, Jason knew that if he showed Blakeley the handwritten note, Blakeley would deny having ever seen it. It would be easy to do so. There was no name on the note, only initials. Why would Blakeley admit to such?

Several times throughout the day, Lonn Trost asked Jason to speak louder. At one point Trost jokingly said, "You wouldn't make it across the street in this city." This irritated Jason, but it appeared that the kid from Arkansas was building a strong case against the New Yorkers and not from being loud and brazen but from quiet confidence and impeccable preparation.

As everyone was packing their belongings to leave, Jason and Rich Rabin had a casual conversation in which Rabin told Jason of several places he should visit while in New York. The depositions had ended earlier than the previous days, so Rabin must have known it would give Jason an opportunity to see a variety of attractions. Jason knew, despite a few actions during the depositions to the contrary, that Rabin was a good guy. He even thought to himself how much he would like to sit down and have a beer with Rabin and maybe talk baseball outside of this particular arena. Rabin was simply doing his job. Jason would have taken a similar approach in the matter if the tables were turned. Rabin might have attempted to paint Jason's client and Oquendo as something other than what they truly were, but Jason knew deep down that Rabin was a quality person and one hell of a lawyer.

Jason walked by himself from the Commissioner's office back to his hotel. He was still in awe over the fact that he had just wrapped up depositions against the New York Yankees. Here he was, walking alongside people on the streets of Manhattan who had no idea that the attorney from Arkansas was giving their premier professional sports team everything they could handle.

That evening, Jason and Oquendo had dinner together in the hotel. Dinner concluded relatively early, so afterwards the two walked to a pub just down the street from their hotel. Jason ordered a Heineken and Oquendo pulled out two cigars…Cuban. Oquendo said, "I'm honestly surprised that anyone took this case, considering the power the Yankees have within Major League Baseball. Actually, I'm surprised that Ricalde pushed the case this far."

"I think Ricalde considered the Yankees' actions a slap in the face and that's why he pursued the case," Jason said.

The two continued to sit on the side patio with New York bustling around them, discussing the case and relaxing from the long three days of depositions. This part of the unique journey was over.

After Jason returned to Arkansas from New York, he received a call from Oquendo. Oquendo had spoken with Lou Melendez in the Commissioner's office and the prevailing attitude within their office was that nearly everyone was disappointed in Gordon Blakeley's testimony during the depositions. They were surprised at how little Blakeley could recall regarding the case.

CHAPTER 9

"It ain't over 'til it's over."
– Yogi Berra

Two weeks later, after both sides had a chance to study the information gathered during the depositions, Rich Rabin filed a second motion for dismissal with the Commissioner's office on behalf of the New York Yankees.

To this twenty-eight page motion were attached forty-three exhibits covering approximately one hundred and fifty pages that the Yankees hoped would support the motion. A large portion of the motion was an attempt to dismiss and discredit testimony given by the Yucatan Lions' witnesses.

A sentence within the first page of the motion gave a prelude to their strategy: *"As set forth below, the Yankees have established - through the Lions' own sworn testimony – that the Lions' claims are based on a document containing false terms, which is not what it purports to be, and which is unenforceable on its face."*

The Yankees were now claiming the contract in question was not only unenforceable but fraudulent (a term that is used throughout the motion). The first page concluded with this suggestion: *"The Yankees now have expended considerable time and money defending against admitted falsehoods and resisting veiled threats by the Lions. This case should be dismissed immediately, and the Yankees should be awarded all of their fees and costs in connection with defending it."*

As Jason read through the motion, he knew the Yankees had set forth all their energy in getting the grievance dismissed before a hearing could be scheduled. He sensed that the motion he held in his hand was well drafted, and that the Yankees felt secure enough with their arguments that the Commissioner would have no other alternative but to dismiss the grievance.

Within the motion there were attacks on several apparent discrepancies in the testimony of the Lions witnesses. Three such examples follow:

• Sr. Ricalde claimed the alleged negotiations lasted "a couple of hours." By contrast, Mr. Oquendo claimed the alleged negotiations were extremely brief, lasting a mere five to ten minutes after the men left the ballpark.

• Sr. Ricalde claimed it took less than twenty minutes to type the alleged agreement. By contrast, Mr. Oquendo claimed that almost three hours elapsed between the conclusion of negotiations and Sr. Ricalde's arrival at the hotel with the typed contract.

• Sr. Ricalde claimed that the alleged agreement was executed around 8:30 or 9:30 p.m. By contrast, Mr. Oquendo claimed that Sr. Ricalde did not even arrive at the hotel until "the wee hours of night, very late at night."

These things were irrelevant to the real issue at hand: the contract and whether or not it allowed Yucatan to collect on the $500,000. Throughout the motion, countless trivial arguments did nothing but attempt to deflect attention from their contractual obligation.

On page four of the motion for dismissal, the Yankees' stated: *"The Lions also have committed other egregious acts in pursuing this bogus claim. Since the beginning of this action, the Lions have threatened to publicize these proceedings and/or bring allegedly "sensitive" issues to the Commissioner's attention if the Yankees did not agree to settle this action on terms acceptable to the Lions."* Jason was furious at such a statement. It was completely false, and he viewed it as a desperate and unnecessary attempt to discredit him as Yucatan's attorney.

Jason gave careful thought to his response and answered this claim by saying: *"No threats were made and absolutely no settlement discussions were broached by Yucatan as of July 8, 2004, or any other time during this process. Yucatan challenges the Yankees to provide any documents, phone logs (recordings), or correspondence from Yucatan that demand payment in return for a release of all claims. It is imperative to note that absolutely no settlement demands have ever been made during these proceedings."*

On page five of the motion the Yankees seemed to hurt their case by reiterating the fact that the Commissioner of Major League Baseball had already denied their first attempt to have the case dismissed when they said: *"The Yankees repeatedly have advised the Commissioner's office that this matter was nothing more than a shakedown. The Yankees have referred this matter to Baseball Security on at least three different occasions, and have sought dismissal of this baseless suit."*

However, Commissioner Selig felt there was enough evidence to continue towards a hearing.

Yet another argument the Yankees made was one that involved a settlement made in March of 2003 with the United States Office of Foreign Assets Control (OFAC) regarding their dealing with Michel Hernández. The Yankees attempted to make a case that because the Commissioner's office decided against any monetary penalties and because a settlement was reached with OFAC, there must have been no wrongdoing in this case.

Once again, these statements had no bearing on the enforcement of the contract between the Yankees and the Yucatan Lions. The following is the actual wording from the Yankees' motion for dismissal: *"...the Commissioner determined that the Yankees did not commit any Rules violations in connection with Mr. Hernández' signing, and the Commissioner declined to assess any penalties against the Yankees. In addition, the Yankees voluntarily have submitted information concerning these events to the Office of Foreign Assets Control ("OFAC") and, in March 2003, reached a settlement with OFAC regarding the incidental expenses incurred by the Yankees on behalf of the player. The facts material to the Lions' claims thus now have been presented not only to the Commissioner's office, but to the federal government as well."*

Jason stated in his response: *"The fact that the Yankees may have voluntarily or involuntarily, settled with OFAC regarding certain compliance (or non-compliance) issues pertaining to the Cuban Assets Control Regulations (CACR), bears no relevance to the present agreement at issue. Even if the Yankees paid the Department of Treasury an informal settlement amount to absolve them of any wrongdoing with their subsequent dealings with Mr. Hernández (or any other Cubans), it does not satisfy the Yankees' obligation to Yucatan.*

*This is yet another flawed and misguided attempt to convince
Major League Baseball that the Club's post-1996 activities
absolved them of their contractual obligations. The informal
settlement did not encompass what transpired before Mr.
Hernández signed in 1998, much less the events that transpired
in Merida, Mexico, in November 1996."*

On pages six and seven of the Yankees' motion, there
were four paragraphs that discussed the events surrounding their
supposed first notification of the existence of the contract with
the Lions. They claimed that was the first they had ever heard of
the contract. Jorge Oquendo, who was no longer an employee of
the Yankees, telephoned Jean Afterman, the Yankees' Assistant
General Manager on November 26, 2002 to discuss the
document. In the Yankees' motion they said: *"Mr. Oquendo's
telephone call raised immediate concerns of potential fraud.
The alleged agreement at issue was more than six years old,
and no one in the Yankees organization had ever heard of it or
seen it."*

That statement, in itself, could be understandable if, in
fact, this was the first the Yankees had heard of the contract.
But the reasoning as to why the call from Oquendo seemed odd
was itself strange. The Yankees claimed that Oquendo acted
"agitated" during the phone call. They said: *"In sum, from the
outset, Mr. Oquendo acted as if the alleged agreement was a
fraud, heightening suspicions within the Yankees
organization... Oquendo was convinced that the Yankees would
not pay the amount allegedly due."*

The fact that the Yankees termed Oquendo's actions suspicious and his demeanor agitated was not only highly subjective but wholly self-serving and groundless.

In the next paragraph, the Yankees explained that following the phone call from Oquendo and following the subsequent request for payment by Yucatan counsel, they referred the matter to Kevin Hallinan, Director of Security for Major League Baseball. In the final sentence in this paragraph the Yankees state that *"...Baseball Security declined to investigate the authenticity of the document."* The head of Baseball's own security department did not wish to investigate. Perhaps this was because Hallinan did not see any evidence to act otherwise.

A major part of the Yankees' strategy was to question Jorge Oquendo's authority to sign the contract. They questioned Yucatan's claim that Oquendo was, at the time of the contract signing, the Coordinator of Scouting for Latin America. They claimed that Oquendo was simply an area scout who earned a mere $12,000 in 1996 and that he was never authorized to sign contracts for the Yankees. Throughout the motion for dismissal, the Yankees downplayed Oquendo's role in their organization.

Jason answered each point of the claims: *"Another attempt by the Yankees to challenge the existence of the Yucatan/Yankees agreement was their argument that Mr. Oquendo was a "part time scout" from November 15, 1994, through 1995 and a full time scout in 1996 with various ranges of compensation. The compensation that other Yankees scouts may have earned in those respective years does not have any bearing on the absolute and undisputed fact that the only reason Mr. Blakeley flew to Merida was because Mr. Oquendo called him and informed him of Hernández' defection."*

Jason also pointed out in his response that *"Although the Yankees deem it 'ludicrous' that Mr. Oquendo was the 'boss' or coordinator over the more senior and higher paid scouts, such conveniently overlooks the significant fact that it was Mr. Oquendo who took the phone call from Carlos Paz (the scout in Mexico), and in turn, called Mr. Blakeley about Mr. Hernández' defection. It is worth noting that Mr. Blakeley was surely motivated to see a player he did not know the name of upon notice from such an 'underling' as Mr. Oquendo."*

Whether or not Oquendo held the title that Yucatan's counsel claimed is irrelevant. The important issue remained: Gordon Blakeley, a high ranking Yankees' employee, apparently felt Oquendo was important enough that he immediately boarded a plane bound for Mexico after speaking with Oquendo.

The next item on the Yankees' motion simply showed the organization's egocentrism. The Yankees stated that the contract was written in Spanish: *"Every other agreement between the Yankees and Lions is written in English (so that the Yankees could understand what it was they were signing)."*

They even went as far as to question the letterhead. The Yankees said of the contract paper: *"The document is written on Lions letterhead with a large 'Leones de Yucatan' logo and a special footer. This letterhead is notably different than the Lions letterhead used in an accounting agreement that actually was*

*executed by the parties on November 4, 1996... The alleged
agreement also is written in a different typeface than the
accounting agreement executed on November 4, 1996."*

The Yankees spent the next three pages arguing about
the discrepancy over the date the contract was signed. They also
questioned the validity of the notary's signature and seal. Every
part of the contract was questioned except for the validity of its
contents. The Yankees' counsel was silent about the actual
content of the contract.

After these side trips, the Yankees returned to the
question of whether Oquendo had the authority to sign the
contract on their behalf. In the past, a man who held the same
position as Oquendo had signed contracts on behalf of the
Yankees. His name was Rudy Santin. Ricalde signed several
agreements with Santin and some of these came to fruition,
therefore Ricalde never questioned Santin's authority to sign the
agreements for the Yankees.

The Yankees continued their attack on Oquendo:
*"According to Mr. Oquendo's own scouting report, the player
had an OFP of [average], which is a "C" player. A "C" player
is nothing more than an "average everyday player," such as a
catcher with "limited offensive production" or a "4-5 starter."
Even apart from all the other evidence as noted above, this
scouting report is all but fatal to the Lions' claim, as it belies
any motive the Yankees could have had to enter into the alleged
agreement."* This statement makes one wonder why the
Yankees would have called Gus Dominguez to make sure

Hernández was taken from Mexico and eventually housed at the Yankees baseball academy in Venezuela.

In 1996, Hernández's talents were well-documented. Perhaps the Yankees, in their disappointment that Hernández never became the star they had hoped for, downplayed the player's talents eight years later in an attempt to rid themselves of a bad investment.

Jason's response to the motion for dismissal touched on other specific subjects not discussed in the Yankees' motion. One of the most interesting surrounded the testimony of Gordon Blakeley. Mr. Blakeley had trouble recalling details surrounding his trip to Mexico to evaluate Hernández.

Page fourteen of Jason's response spoke to this: *"Mr. Blakeley's testimony as to what Mr. Hernández's 'practice' consisted of and with whom is telling of his questionable veracity. Although Mr. Blakeley does not recall when he arrived at the Lion's stadium, he seemed to emphatically recall Mr. Hernández practicing with the Lions Baseball Club. When specifically asked if Michel Hernández was subject to a workout when Mr. Blakeley was in Mexico, Mr. Blakeley unequivocally testified: 'Michel Hernández was practicing with the Lions team.' Not disputing that Mr. Blakeley's trip to Mexico was in November of 1996, it was not possible for Mr. Hernández to have practiced with the Yucatan Lions team at such time. Simply the team was not together during the off-season. In 1996, the Lions season ended in August."*

Ricalde testified that Carlos Paz instructed him to make sure no press knew of the Yankees' visit and the subsequent workout. They did not want anyone knowing that an executive from the Yankees was checking out the ball player. It was a private workout for only the Yankees' representatives to see.

Jason concluded his response by reacting to the Yankees' assertion that Yucatan was to blame for this drawn out, two-year-long process. He wrote: *"It was the Yankees who filed a meritless Motion to Dismiss on October 1, 2003. A preliminary discovery schedule was discussed as of June 2003, only four months after Mr. Cashman was put on notice of the agreement. It was the Yankees who extended this process by filing a Motion to Dismiss and, in turn, were compelled to conduct discovery. The Yankees have not endured anything other than being confronted with the truth surrounding the transaction, and that, indeed, Mr. Blakeley participated in the handling of a Cuban defector from Mexico to Venezuela and then to the United States."*

Finally, Jason quoted Blakeley from his testimony, which speaks volumes as to why he might take such a risk: *"I work for an owner that's very competitive. And we try to get the best players. We don't always succeed. If we do not get a particular player, we need to be able to justify why we didn't get the player."* This was a brief Jason worked on for at least four days off-and-on. Not knowing the tenor of Bud Selig, he was worried about the tone of his arguments. He was adamant his client was right (like any litigator, he lost most, if not all sense of objectivity), but he didn't want to over-sell his position. When finally satisfied by the tone, he sent the brief to Commissioner Selig and Rabin. Jason couldn't help but think that placing the stamp on the outgoing envelope could be his last act in this grievance. The motion prepared by the Yankees, if accepted, could have ended the grievance, without further action. It was imperative to Jason that the Yankees' motion be denied.

On August 26, 2005, Bud Selig signed a letter addressed to the Yankees and the Yucatan Lions. In this letter, Selig rendered his decision, as arbitrator, on the Yankees' motion for dismissal. After reviewing the details of the case, Selig said: *"On March 22, 2004, I denied a motion to dismiss that the Yankees had filed, concluding that, after assuming the Lions' allegations to be true, the Yankees were not entitled to prevail. The Yankees have since made a second motion to dismiss, relying on certain testimony developed in the course of the grievance. The parties have also each moved for discovery-related sanctions against the other. After careful consideration of all of the information submitted by the parties to this dispute, I deny the Yankees' renewed motion to dismiss and reserve final decision on the sanctions motions."*

Selig went on to say: *"Considering the disputed evidence in the Yucatan Club's favor, as I must, one may conclude that an employee of the Yankees with the authority to bind the Yankees made an agreement with the Yucatan Club to compensate the Yucatan Club for services rendered to the Yankees. Whether that was actually the case remains to be seen, but I cannot now conclude, on the basis of the written submissions made, that the Yankees must necessarily prevail in the face of disputed evidence that an enforceable agreement was made. The Yankees also contend that the alleged agreement's inaccurate date and notarization renders it invalid. Those issues, however, go to the credibility of the Yucatan Club's evidence and do not demonstrate that the alleged agreement cannot under any circumstances be enforceable."*

Selig concluded by saying: *"Resolving all disputed facts in favor of the Yucatan Club, I cannot conclude that the Yankees are entitled to prevail in this grievance. Material facts are in dispute. The Yankees, in their closing arguments, may make the arguments they have advanced about the credibility of the evidence, but they are not now entitled to prevail in the dispute. This matter will be set for a hearing. No further dispositive motions will be entertained."*

Selig would not dismiss the case. It would go forward. Jason was elated! The case would finally go to hearing and Selig would personally serve as arbitrator. Or so Jason thought...

Later that same year, Selig replaced himself as arbitrator with Bob DuPuy. Selig was busy dealing with challenges on two fronts. The first was the steroid issue. In 2005, Congressional hearings were held in Washington, D.C. to determine the extent to which performance enhancing drugs were being used in professional baseball. Sammy Sosa and Mark McGwire were among several active and retired Major League Baseball players to testify. The pressure brought on Major League Baseball following these hearings forced Selig to spend much of 2005 dealing with baseball's collective bargaining agreement in regards to drug testing of the athletes.

The second issue that distracted Selig from the
Yankees/Lions case was the negotiations with DirecTV over the
rights to carry Extra Innings, a package baseball fans could
purchase to watch multiple out-of-market Major League
Baseball games through the satellite TV provider.

Jason was comfortable with DuPuy serving as arbitrator
because DuPuy was a fellow attorney, but efforts by Jason to
get the Yankees to the grievance table would prove futile.

In the months following Selig's letter, Jason called Ed
Burns at the Commissioner's office multiple times in an attempt
to set a date for the hearing. Señor Ricalde's attention was now
directed towards battling cancer and with his health diminishing
and his impatience growing, Jason knew he needed to set a
hearing date as quickly as possible.

Jason called Ed Burn's office so often that after several
weeks, Jason could have sworn he heard giggles from Burn's
secretary when he called. It was as if she tried to tell him,
"Yeah, sure, go ahead and hold your breath waiting for him to
call you back."

The case seemed to be fading away and with no notable
progress, so Jason sent another letter to Bob DuPuy voicing his
frustration that no hearing had been scheduled. At the very
least, Jason was trying to keep the dialogue open. He refused to
let the case die. At the Winter Meetings in Dallas, in December
2005, Jason had been told that a hearing could be conducted
between January 20th and 31st, 2006. Jason knew Oquendo
could fly in any time and he believed that he could convince
Ricalde to participate. Even if Ricalde declined, Jason knew he

had the deposition tapes that could be used in Ricalde's absence. Jason agreed to the January dates but held off on making any reservations; rightfully so, the hearing never came to fruition.

On January 3, 2006, Rich Rabin sent a letter to Bob DuPuy saying the Yankees wanted to resolve this issue quickly and recommended each side submit a brief to the Commissioner's office instead of reconvening for a hearing. Jason felt this request was ludicrous. Two days later he responded to Rabin's letter by notifying DuPuy that Yucatan should be afforded a hearing; he referenced Commissioner Selig's decision to deny the Yankees second motion for dismissal.

On January 9th, Rabin responded by saying that all along the Commissioner's office had left open the manner in which the dispute would be presented to the Commissioner and that there had been no manner yet determined. He said the videotaped depositions and other documentation gathered during the discovery process should be enough to submit to the Commissioner for a decision. Otherwise, he said, they would be going over the same ground and it would be unproductive.

With his frustration mounting, Jason fired off a response reiterating that the Commissioner himself said, "*...this matter will be set for a hearing.*" Jason stated a hearing should not be dismissed simply out of convenience and time consumption. He also mentioned Joe Cubas had not yet been deposed and Jason wanted Cubas as a possible rebuttal witness.

No exchanges were made over the next three weeks, but on January 30th Jason sent a letter to Rabin expressing his frustration over the Yankees' refusal to participate in a hearing. He said: *"I was unaware the Yankees would have an opportunity to dictate the procedural aspect without consideration for my client, much less Commissioner Selig's directive that a hearing be set."* Jason recommended mediation as an alternative, stating, *"Submitting this matter by brief is not an optimal approach, and indeed not acceptable to Yucatan."*

Jason then informed the Commissioner's office that he and his witnesses would be available for a hearing February 16th and 17th but was told the Yankees did not respond. Jason hoped this would be resolved by Opening Day of the 2006 Major League Baseball season. Rabin again stated, in a letter to Bob DuPuy on February 23rd, that the case was "baseless" and that considerable time and resources had been wasted over the past three years defending the case. Again he requested that the case be submitted via brief.

On April 12th, Jason sent another letter to DuPuy expressing frustration at the hearing process. He stated: *"Given the time that has elapsed from the onset of the grievance and the repeated requests for hearing dates, if a hearing is not set for final consideration and ruling on the issues, Yucatan may explore other avenues to achieve a necessary resolution."*

Throughout May 2006, many emails were sent by Jason to DuPuy, Ed Burns, Joe Cubas and Señor Ricalde via Alex Escalante to try to schedule a hearing in either June or July with no result. Jason's frustrations were fast approaching a boiling point.

During the first week in July, Jason sent word to Ricalde that he had learned from Ed Burns that a meeting scheduled between Bob DuPuy and the Yankees to discuss this matter was cancelled, but that Burns would try to stay on DuPuy to reschedule. This email contained the first mention of a possible settlement. This excited Jason. Maybe this case would be resolved in the near future! He knew Ricalde was running out of time and patience.

Jason sent another letter to DuPuy in September 2006 stating that the correspondence signed by both parties acknowledging that DuPuy would take over for Selig as the arbitrator in this dispute was now five months old, and a hearing had yet to be set. He again recommended mediation.

In November, nearly a year after he was told at the Winter Meetings that a hearing would be scheduled, Jason emailed Ed Burns about the possibility of setting a meeting at the upcoming Winter Meetings to serve as a "mediation-like" scenario, but still there was nothing set. He began entertaining different approaches to get the Yankees to the table.

In December 2006, Jason attended the MLB Winter Meetings, this time in Orlando. It was now four years after his original conversation with Señor Ricalde in Tennessee. His main objective was to meet with the President of the Mexican Baseball League, Plinio Escalante. Jason hoped that Escalante would help him in his quest to get the attention of the Commissioner's office. After all, the team he represented was a member of the Mexican League, so Jason felt that Escalante would have an interest in the case. Though Escalante was very gracious with his time and listened to Jason's request, Escalante responded that, unfortunately, he would not be able to help. Jason was disappointed. He had hoped this meeting might reveal a new path in his journey, but now Jason knew he must continue down the road he had traveled for over four years.

Finally, in April of 2007 and nearly two and a half years after the Yankees' last motion for dismissal, Jason received an email from Ed Burns that asked how much money it would take to settle the case. Either the Commissioner's office was simply tired of the case and Jason's persistence, or the Yankees were so obstinate on this issue and their refusal to commit to a date that the Commissioner's office thought that they might have better luck with a settlement.

Notwithstanding the Yankees' defense to the grievance, it always perplexed Jason that Commissioner Selig charged that a hearing would be scheduled, but absolutely nothing was done to coordinate it short of floating some dates around. What was the purpose of informing the clubs a hearing would be scheduled if the Yankees absolute refusal would override the Commissioner?

Jason emailed Rich Rabin on April 14th to ask if he had discussed the possibility of a settlement with the Yankees. To Jason's surprise and disappointment (again) Rabin said he knew nothing about it but would check with the Yankees. It was the last correspondence Jason would receive from Rich Rabin on this issue.

On April 26th, Jason wrote to DuPuy to check the status of the settlement process. He stated: *"It is reasonable for Yucatan to deem the continuous failure to respond to its inquiries as a rejection of such terms... I believe it is apparent Yucatan is going to continue to push for a resolution or at least some affirmative movement rather than allow the grievance to be stalled in perpetuity."*

The first week of May, Jason was informed by Ed Burns that Jason was now to communicate directly with MLB regarding the case. Apparently, the Yankees no longer wanted to pay for an attorney's services on this case. Jason was baffled. It was as if the entire case was simply being ignored, and with the Yankees' attorneys now out of the picture, Jason wondered just who he would deal with now.

Jason informed Burns that he would be in New York for an unrelated matter the following month. He decided it would be difficult for the Commissioner's office to say no to a meeting since he was coming to them. If the Yankees refused to be a part of the resolution, Jason would press the Commissioner's office for a possible alternative. Burns agreed to set a meeting for Jason with Bob DuPuy during the time Jason would be in New York.

The day of the meeting in June 2007, Jason went to the Commissioner's office with the feeling that he was once again about to be "blown off." He was skeptical that the meeting would even take place, much less that an agreement would be reached on a settlement. He imagined that he would arrive and be told that Bob DuPuy was called out of town on other business, but DuPuy's secretary escorted Jason to a conference room and said that Mr. DuPuy would be in soon.

Jason sat quietly in the conference room admiring the photographs of various United States Presidents who had thrown out a first pitch at an MLB game. After about twenty minutes, Ed Burns entered the room flanked by Bob DuPuy and Jimmie Lee Solomon, the Executive Vice President of Baseball Operations. Jason was familiar with Solomon, but he had never actually met the man.

Solomon had been working hard in recent years to revitalize baseball within the nation's inner-cities. Solomon also was instrumental in forming the Civil Rights Game that was scheduled to be played in Memphis beginning in 2007 to commemorate and celebrate Martin Luther King. Jason was surprised to see Solomon at the meeting since he had not been involved in the case up to that point, at least to Jason's understanding.

Certain parameters of a settlement had already been discussed with Ed Burns via email over the previous weeks, and Jason hoped this meeting would confirm the terms and provide him the assurance the grievance would indeed be resolved by a certain date. It was not long after the brief introductions that DuPuy said that the matter would be resolved and finalized to the satisfaction of Yucatan by June 15th.

Though not completely happy with the terms of the settlement, Jason was content. Jason and Ricalde felt this might be their last opportunity for any semblance of a positive outcome. There might be no future offers and Jason was instructed by Ricalde prior to the meeting to accept any reasonable settlement.

Once the settlement talks were concluded, the men engaged in a bit of light banter, and DuPuy asked Jason about the Arkansas Naturals, the new double-A team in the Kansas City Royals farm system that was being formed in Northwest Arkansas. DuPuy and Solomon then excused themselves. Ed Burns stayed to continue the conversation and the discussion turned to the Mexican League, whose president Jason had recently met, and to the relationship it had with MLB.

The conversation then shifted to Major League Baseball's expansion efforts into China. Burns told Jason of a recent trip to China where he and several others from Major League Baseball examined several baseball facilities there and discussed expansion options with several Chinese heads of state. Jason could not believe he was sitting in the Commissioner's office, discussing such matters. It was all a bit too surreal for him, but he felt comfort in knowing he had accomplished his mission in New York.

Burns wrapped up the casual conversation by asking if Jason planned to attend the New York Yankees / Boston Red Sox game at Yankee Stadium that evening. Jason would not pass up the opportunity to attend perhaps the most storied rivalry in professional sports. He and his wife, who accompanied him to New York had tickets to the game the following evening. Jason couldn't wait. It was his first live Yankees / Red Sox game.

The next night, as Jason and Robin enjoyed the game sitting next to the Red Sox dugout, Jason's Blackberry vibrated in his pocket. Jason looked to see Ed Burns had emailed a copy of the settlement agreement during the Yankees' game. "How surreal," Jason thought, while reading the terms of a settlement involving the very team he was watching. Given how long it took to achieve a resolution, Jason was encouraged by how quickly Burns had prepared the settlement agreement. He believed he had accomplished what he set out to by scheduling the meeting in New York. He also took satisfaction in the Red Sox win that night.

As the settlement date grew closer, Jason's feelings of encouragement were being replaced with doubt. He had not seen a copy of the agreement signed by the Yankees and was unsure of whether the Yankees had agreed upon the terms as drafted by Ed Burns. All Jason had to go on was DuPuy's assurance that the terms of settlement would be satisfied by that date.

On June fifteenth, Jason traveled to Little Rock for depositions on another matter. With no verification that the terms of settlement had been met, Jason called Ed Burns on his drive to Little Rock. Burns took Jason's call and advised him he was going to have to look into the situation. He asked Jason to call him later that afternoon and hoped to have an answer.

Just as asked, Jason called Burns on his way back home after the depositions. It was during this call that Jason learned the Yankees were not going to satisfy the terms of settlement, and undoubtedly were not going to adhere to its obligations by the deadline. Sensing Jason's frustration, Burns informed him that MLB would meet the settlement terms, but it could not be accomplished until a date after the fifteenth. The Yankees, notably absent the last couple of years, were yet again in no way involved in the settlement. The Commissioner's office was going to foot the bill for the Yankees rather than force them to hold a hearing or to settle the dispute. Jason knew it probably would not matter to Ricalde who paid the money, but Jason knew this was out of the norm, perhaps even a conflict of interest.

Jason was not sure what the interplay was like between the Yankees and the Commissioner's office regarding the settlement, but it really was no surprise to him that the Yankees were not going to be participants in the resolution with Yucatan. After all, the Yankees had effectively withdrawn after Selig's order denying the Yankees' request for dismissal. Perhaps the Commissioner's office was put in the unenviable position of needing to achieve a resolution to the grievance but getting absolutely no support from the Yankees in doing so. Yet, from Jason's perspective, getting it resolved was paramount because Señor Ricalde had grown very ill by this time, and the thought of prolonging the grievance process was not palatable.

To this day questions still remain regarding whether or not the Yankees ever knew of the terms of settlement or actually saw the settlement agreement. For all Jason knows, the Yankees never knew of his meeting with DuPuy in May 2007. Did the Yankees adhere to their defense and refuse to participate in the settlement, thus leaving Major League Baseball with such an obligation? Was Jason's persistence in seeking a hearing enough to compel MLB to resolve it just so Yucatan would go away? Why would Selig charge that the grievance would go to a hearing but then never schedule one?

Whatever the relationship between the Yankees and the Commissioner's office might have been before, during, or even after the grievance, the Commissioner had the authority to fine any Major League club up to two million dollars and an owner, officer or employee up to $500,000 pursuant to the Major League Constitution for dealing with Cuban players. The Major League Constitution gives the Commissioner power to investigate any act, transaction, or practice charged, alleged or suggested not to be in the best interest of baseball, and to determine the preventive, remedial or punitive action that is appropriate. The facts developed during the Yucatan grievance process made Jason consider this rule, and he wondered if the actions of the Yankees would compel Selig to enforce it, but that never happened.

In 1999, precedent had been set when the Los Angeles Dodgers were deemed to have violated Major League Rules by scouting in Cuba. Then, the Dodgers lost their contractual rights to two Cuban players, and the Dodgers were fined $200,000. The circumstances that compelled Selig to exert his authority against the Dodgers were almost parallel to the situation with Michel Hernández. Jason thought, no doubt naively, that since a member club of the National Association of Professional Baseball Leagues was responsible for bringing the issue of Michel's defection to the Commissioner's attention,

Selig wanted the facts developed and was using Jason's representation of Yucatan as the mechanism to bringing the issues to light. After all, Selig denied the Yankees' multiple attempts to dismiss the grievance and charged that Yucatan's claim would go to hearing.

However, the substance and subject matter that made up the grievance and the facts giving rise to the contract at issue raised a more complex concern for Jason. This concern was for the player, Hernández. Jason had no doubt Hernández would have never left Mexico with the Yankees had it not been for the contract between Yucatan and the Yankees. Yet, he was also uneasy with the thought that Hernández might not have been afforded free agency because the Yankees were the first and only team to be called when he defected. This uneasiness lingered despite a previous ruling from Selig in a separate grievance that acknowledged Hernandez's failed attempts to void his contract with the Yankees. Jason was led to believe that Hernandez, having been represented by his agent at the time, Joe Cubas, participated in a full hearing to determine his free agent status in 1999. The complexity of the situation arose when the evidence Jason presented on Yucatan's behalf proved otherwise. Nonetheless, Jason, along with the Commissioner, considered the grievance to be a club versus club issue, so Jason took some solace in the thought there was nothing this grievance could do to jeopardize Hernández's status with any club with which he would be affiliated.

Although the case had a rather unexpected and anticlimactic conclusion, Senor Ricalde was satisfied with the outcome. He was fast approaching the end and had a mere few months of life remaining. The way the case ended left Jason with an unsatisfied feeling, a feeling of business unfinished. Jason did not feel like he had 'won,' but the fact that Ricalde was happy somehow made it more palatable. He often imagined what it would have been like if this case had made it to a hearing. What else might he have discovered if it had?

This long and meandering odyssey might have begun eleven years before in Mexico with the defection of Michel Hernández, but he was not entitled to any part of the settlement. The contract at the center of this case was between the Yucatan Lions and the New York Yankees. Unfortunately, it was never about the player who started it all, who risked his life in pursuit of his freedom and his dream to play baseball in America. Hernández was an asset in a game played every day throughout the world. In the world of international baseball scouting there will undoubtedly be an endless supply of players like Hernández to be bought and sold and tossed aside when they reach the end of their usefulness, each playing a small part in filling the coffers of those who control the game.

After the grievance was concluded, Jason had an opportunity to speak with Michel Hernández, and many of the facts of this story, detailed from Michel's perspective, were verified mirroring Jorge Oquendo's testimony. He said he was first introduced to Gordon Blakeley and Jorge Oquendo at the Lions' stadium in Merida, Yucatan, where he was put through a workout, by himself, and not with the Yucatan team. After the workout, Michel was taken to the Fiesta Americana hotel and was given food and adequate clothing. A few days later, Michel was introduced to Ken Dominguez, and Ken escorted Michel, who without documentation used the name Juan, Ken Dominguez' cousin, to Mexico City. There, Ken Dominguez introduced Michel to Angel Santos, an agent, who had instructions to escort Michel to Venezuela. Using a false passport provided by Angel Santos, Michel was transported to Caracas, Venezuela on December 24, 1996. Michel was first introduced to Gus Dominguez on August 18, 1997 while he lived in Venezuela, and as told by Michel, it was Gus Dominguez who worked to get the Yankees to remain interested in his services. Gordon Blakeley even visited Michel while in Venezuela to check on his conditioning and to inform him of his potential assignment to the Yankees' minor league affiliates. At no time did Michel have knowledge that Gus Dominguez and Angel Santos had a working relationship with Gordon Blakeley, or that it was Blakeley that called Gus Dominguez shortly after Michel's workout in Mexico.

It was in Venezuela that the Yankees presented a minor league contract for him to sign, at the urging of Raul Ortega, the Yankees' representative in Venezuela. Michel did so without his agents, Gus Dominguez or Angel Santos present. He was still a Cuban citizen at the time he signed, and was in Venezuela only with an emergency passport and foreign temporary resident status. A few days after signing with the Yankees, Michel was taken to Valencia, Venezuela, where the Yankees' baseball academy was located.

Michel felt as if he fled one regime only to be bound by
another, the Yankees. Though shy and soft-spoken, Michel
made it obvious to Jason that he never truly felt free after his
defection, and that he was denied an open market that would
have been available had he been a true free agent. His pleas are
evident in a letter he wrote in 1999 to Bill Murray, then Director
of Operations for Major League Baseball. Michel hoped to have
his contract with the Yankees voided and to be granted free
agency. After he learned more of the Yankees and Gus
Dominguez' collaborative efforts regarding his contract with the
Yankees organization, he wrote: *"At this moment I am tired to
knocking doors in different places, lawyers, immigration offices
and the proceedings are at great length with not a fast solution
to my serious problem. This must be lack of observation,
patience and serenity of all responsible parties. I am a Cuban
baseball player, that only was looking for freedom and on
baseball I saw that opportunity, and now I feel a slave of the
New York Yankees... "* These pleas fell on deaf ears.

In a June 12, 2003 letter from Richard L. "Sandy"
Alderson, then Executive Vice President, Baseball Operations
for MLB, Michel was informed that the Commissioner denied
his request for free agency. This was supposedly communicated
to Michel by his agent, Joe Cubas, although Michel denied ever
receiving such notice in 1999. The purpose of Alderson's letter
was to address Michel's renewed concerns about his free agent
status and the true events that gave rise to his contract with the
Yankees. From Alderson, Michel was led to believe that Gus
Dominguez advertised Michel's availability to all Major league

Clubs during the winter of 1997-1998. Alderson's explanation of the denial was apparently premised on statements made by Gus Dominguez that at least two Major League clubs made offers but that after a discussion with Michel detailing the offers, Michel agreed, upon Gus Dominguez's recommendation, to sign with the Yankees, a club that Gus Dominguez said offered the highest signing bonus, $60,000. Not surprisingly, neither Gordon Blakeley nor Jorge Oquendo was quizzed by the Commissioner about the circumstances surrounding Michel's contract.

What started out as a letter of inquiry in January 2003 turned into a grievance that spanned four entire seasons, culminating in four different World Series Champions (none of which were the Yankees) that eventually concluded in June 2007. When the grievance started, Jason's son was not yet born. When the grievance was concluded, his son was one month shy of his fourth birthday.

EXTRA INNINGS

Jason Browning

Jason remains a partner at Warner, Smith and Harris where he continues his legal work and maintains a working relationship with his sports agent and friend, Chris Fanta. Despite what the Ricalde case taught him about the darker side of the game, baseball will always be a passion for Jason. What he has seen and experienced on the "business" side of the sport has done nothing to alter his thoughts or feelings for the game. Whenever Jason visits a ballpark to watch a game, he experiences a youthful exuberance. Now he sees the same excitement expressed by his son, Colin, when they walk up the tunnel to the stands to be greeted by all the sights, sounds, and smells of baseball.

It has been many years since Jason put on a uniform and experienced the excitement of roaming the field or taking the mound in a relief effort during a close game. Now that joy and excitement comes from watching his son play. Jason's love of the game is not lost on Colin as he now wears his father's old college number, fourteen. The perfection of the game, at least to Jason, is now personified by Colin and his teammates and their ever-present smiles, their waves to mom and dad while waiting in the on-deck circle as they express their anticipation of batting next, and the parents - even those for the opposing team - cheering when a player makes a spectacular catch or throw.

For Jason it was not about statistics, wins or losses but about playing the game the right way, seeing the skills develop and - above everything else - sharing a very special pastime between father and son.

Gus Dominguez

Perhaps the story of Gus Dominguez is the most notorious of all. Gus was the sports agent who helped get Michel Hernández from Mexico to Venezuela, and many other actions in support of Hernández over the next two years.

In October 2006, Dominguez and four co-defendants were charged, in a fifty-three-count federal indictment, with smuggling Cuban baseball players into the United States. According to testimony, Dominguez paid $225,000 to known drug smugglers to bring five players by boat to Florida and then to transport them to Dominguez's home in California. The alleged driver of the boat and co-conspirator, Ysbel Medina-Santos ("Javier"), struck a deal with federal prosecutors and agreed to testify against Dominguez in return for a lesser sentence.

There were actually two trips arranged by Dominguez. During the first, smugglers attempted to bring twenty-two Cubans into the United States, but the speedboat was intercepted by authorities just six miles outside of U.S. waters. Nineteen Cubans were in the boat during the next trip a month later, including five baseball players. This attempt was a success, and the Cubans were unloaded on to a desolate beach in the Florida Keys. All of those on the successful voyage were on board the first, unsuccessful attempt.

The strangest aspect of the case was how Dominguez obtained the $225,000 to pay the smugglers. He supposedly funneled the money through the bank account of client, and Major League Baseball player, Henry Blanco. Blanco said he did not know that Dominguez was using his money to pay the smugglers, but Blanco said, "I signed with Gus [Dominguez] because of what other players told me. One said, 'He might not be the best businessman, but he's the best guy. You can trust him with your money and your wife.' And you can."

Many familiar with the case questioned Dominguez's selection of players. Most were not considered good enough to command a high enough Major League Baseball salary to make the smuggling risk worthwhile for Dominguez. None of the five had ever been selected for Cuba's national team. Three of them, Allen Guevara, Osmany Masso, and Yoankis Turino received little interest within American baseball circles. The other two players signed only minor league contracts. In 2007, Osbek Castillo pitched for the Mobile Baybears, the Double-A affiliate of the Arizona Diamondbacks, and Francisley Bueno played for the Mississippi Braves, the Atlanta Braves' Double-A affiliate.

In 2004, Dominguez had successfully paid to have Seattle Mariners' shortstop Yuniesky Betancourt smuggled to the United States. Betancourt ultimately dumped Dominguez and found another agent just before he signed a $3.8 million dollar deal with the Mariners with incentives totaling more than one million dollars. Therefore, Dominguez never received any money from Betancourt.

It is alleged that Betancourt promised to pay his smugglers five percent of his first Major League Baseball contract, but he never paid a dime. This enraged the smugglers who at first, according to Dominguez, made threats to break Betancourt's legs. Then they made threats against Dominguez and his family if he did not come up with the promised money. This is what spurred Dominguez to pay the smugglers.

Prosecutors questioned these claims by asking why Dominguez never contacted the police or the F.B.I. over the threats. Dominguez countered by stating the he feared for the lives of his family, and he simply wanted the whole thing to go away.

Andy Morales, who was mentioned in the mysterious documents sent to Jorge Oquendo, apparently played a role in providing a safe house for some of the Cuban players brought to America by Dominguez. At the onset of his case, Dominguez claimed that he hadn't heard of the Cuban players in question until he was contacted by Morales. He said Morales told him the players were in Miami and could use his help.

Morales was already on the U.S. Attorney's radar screen. They claimed Morales was with Dominguez' co-conspirator in the player smuggling case, Ysbel Medina-Santos ("Javier"), when Santos was arrested for drug trafficking in 2005 in Chicago. Ysbel Medina-Santos' testimony was the prosecution's main weapon. The testimony of a man who admitted to many criminal acts on the witness stand ultimately sent Dominguez to prison. Neither Andy Morales nor Yuniesky Betancourt, both former clients, ever testified on Dominguez' behalf.

The Key West, Florida, jury found Dominguez guilty on twenty-one federal counts which included conspiracy, smuggling, transporting and harboring illegal Cuban immigrants. Dominguez faced more than two hundred years in prison, but on July 9, 2007, he was sentenced to five years, the mandatory minimum sentence. The judge allowed Dominguez to serve his sentence in the Taft Community Correctional Facility, a minimum security compound located about a hundred miles north of Dominguez's home in California.

Ironically, Dominguez' lawyer, Ben Kuehne, who also represented Al Gore during the 2000-election recount in Palm Beach County, was indicted by the U.S. Department of Justice in Washington, D.C. in February, 2008 for money laundering.

In 2010, Gus Dominguez was released from prison. As of the publishing of this book, he was petitioning the Major League Baseball Players Association to be reinstated as an agent.

Michel Hernández

Michel Hernández was signed as an undrafted free agent by the New York Yankees on May 11, 1998. He stayed in the Yankees minor league system until September 1, 2003, when he debuted with the Yankees on September 6th against the Boston Red Sox by playing as a replacement for catcher Jorge Posada. On September 26th, Hernández made his first career major league start and got his first major league hit against the Baltimore Orioles.

In total, Hernández played in five games during his brief major league stint with the Yankees, going one-for-four at the plate. He was designated for minor league assignment on December 23rd. Hernández was claimed off waivers on January

8, 2004 by the Boston Red Sox but was again claimed off
waivers by the Philadelphia Phillies on March 24th.

Hernández played the entire 2004 season for the
Scranton / Wilkes-Barre Red Barons, the Phillies Triple-A
team. There he played in 77 games and batted .254 with 6 home
runs and 31 RBI's. Following the 2004 season, Hernández was
designated for assignment and the next day became a free agent
when the Phillies failed to offer him a new contract.

On January 18, 2005, Hernández signed a minor league
contract with the San Diego Padres and was invited to spring
training but did not make the Padres team. He was reassigned to
the minors where he spent the 2005 season with the Padre's
Triple-A affiliate, the Portland Beavers. There, in 82 games, he
batted .288 with three home runs. On October 28th, Hernández
opted for minor league free agency. On November 14, he was
signed to a one-year minor league contract by the St. Louis
Cardinals.

Hernández played for the Cardinal's Triple-A affiliate,
the Memphis Redbirds, for the entire 2006 season, where he
played in 90 games and averaged .274 with two home runs.
Hernández was designated for assignment by the Cardinals on
January 29, 2007 and on March 5th was reassigned to minor
league camp and became a free agent.

In 2007, Hernández started the season playing for the
Somerset Patriots in the Independent League, but on June 9th he
signed a minor league contract with the Tampa Bay Devil Rays.
He played the remainder of the 2007 season for the Triple-A
Durham Bulls, where he played in 51 games and batted .276

with four home runs. Following the 2007 season, Hernández again opted for minor league free agency.

On December 21, 2007, Hernández signed a minor league contract with the Pittsburg Pirates and was invited to spring training. On March 22nd, he was cut when Pittsburg decided not to carry a third catcher on their roster and was reassigned to the minor leagues.

In 2008, Hernández played for the Pirates' Triple-A International League affiliate, the Indianapolis Indians. During the 2009 season, Hernández played in 35 games for Tampa Bay Devil Rays where he had 99 hits and a batting average of .242. Hernández was listed in the Baltimore Orioles organization as of February 2010.

Jorge Oquendo

Jorge Oquendo last worked in baseball as a scout for the Chicago White Sox from 2004 to 2007. In November 2010, following a two-year investigation, Oquendo was indicted on federal charges by the U.S. Attorney's office. Oquendo, along with former White Sox scout Victor Mateo and the former director of player personnel, David Wilder, were charged with multiple counts of mail fraud. The three were accused of skimming the signing bonuses of an unnamed number of Latin American players. According to the indictment, the three former White Sox employees would secretly inflate the amount of a player's signing bonus and take kickbacks from the excess.

Oquendo and Wilder were charged with seven counts of mail fraud, while Mateo was charged with three counts.

Gustavo Ricalde

Gustavo Ricalde's team, the Yucatan Lions, finished the 2006 season as champions of the Mexican League, the team's third title since its inception. On January 14, 2008, Ricalde died in Houston, Texas, from complications related to throat cancer he had battled for over a year. Ricalde was instrumental in awarding scholarships to underprivileged youth to continue their studies in Mexico. In addition, he was heavily involved with the Red Cross in the Yucatan.

Not only is Ricalde remembered as the founder of the supermarket chain, Super Más, he was also known for his pro-business stance within Mexico. He was a past president of Concanaco, Mexico's Confederation of the National Chambers of Commerce, founded in 1917. Concanaco is an autonomous organization that aids local Chambers of Commerce in their representation to the Mexican federal government. The organization promotes investment in business opportunities throughout Mexico and helps to promote the tourism industry.

Ricalde is credited with arranging and organizing Pope John Paul II's visit to Mexico in 1993.

George Steinbrenner

George Steinbrenner passed away during the final editing of this book. He will be remembered as a controversial, yet very successful sports team owner. It is difficult to think of another team owner who had such an impact on their sport, not just baseball, but any sport.

Steinbrenner, along with a group of investors, purchased the Yankees in 1973 for $10 million. At the time of his death, the Yankees franchise was valued at over $1.6 billion.

Most everyone is aware of George Steinbrenner, the business man. He was notorious and, many times, controversial as the owner of the Yankees, but that was just one persona. Outside the Yankees' world he was a tireless philanthropist and community champion. "I'm really ninety-five percent Mr. Rogers and only five percent Oscar the Grouch," George Steinbrenner once said of himself.

He gave millions of dollars to a variety of charities throughout the years, often with the understanding that the gifts would be made anonymously. His gifts ranged from setting up a college scholarship for an injured high school football player, whom he read about in the newspaper, to giving $1 million to Virginia Tech University following the unfortunate shootings in 2007.

He founded charitable organizations to benefit the families of policemen and women along with countless donations to benefit his adopted home of Tampa, Florida. His gifts and contributions are too voluminous to list.

Over the years, modeled after Steinbrenner's unforgiving, heavy-handed approach to business, the Yankees organization morphed into its own, separate persona. This was the entity Jason contested, not Steinbrenner himself. By the time this case ended, Steinbrenner had relinquished control of his beloved team to his son, Hal. This has proven to be a successful transition, demonstrated by the Yankees' World Series title in 2009. Hal's more subdued management approach has been quite different from his father's, but then again, there will never be another George Steinbrenner.

Bibliography

Badenhausen, Kurt, Micheal K. Ozanian and Christina Settimi. "Baseball's Most Valuable Teams." Forbes.com. 7 April 2010. <http://www.forbes.com/2010/04/06/most-valuable-baseball-teams-business-sportsmoney-baseball-valuations-10-values.html>

Castro, Ivan. "Cubans Are First to Play Baseball Outside the U.S." suite101.com. 9 Nov. 2009. <http://baseballhistory.suite101.com/article.cfm/a_brief_history_of_cuban_baseball>

Caulfield, Brian. "Together Again." Catholic New York Online. 29 Oct. 1998. <http://www.cny.org/archive/ft/ft102998.htm>

Enders, Eric. "El Pasatiempo Nacional." Ericenders.com. May 2001. <http://www.ericenders.com/cubaball.htm>

Lewis, Michael. "Commie Ball: A Journey to the End of a Revolution." Vanity Fair. July 2008. <http://www.vanityfair.com/politics/features/2008/07/cuban_baseball200807>

Marquis, Christopher. "United States Sends Cuban Athlete Home." NYtimes.com. 8 June 2000. < http://www.nytimes.com/2000/06/08/us/united-states-sends-cuban-athlete-home.html>

Nobles, Charlie. "BASEBALL: Yanks Agree to Terms With Defector." NYtimes.com. 14 Feb. 2001. < http://www.nytimes.com/2001/02/14/sports/baseball-yanks-agree-to-terms-with-defector.html?scp=1&sq=Andy+Morales&st=nyt>

Nobles, Charlie. "Cuban Slugger Makes It to U.S. On Second Try." NYtimes.com. 20 July 2000. < http://www.nytimes.com/2000/07/20/us/cuban-slugger-makes-it-to-us-on-second-try.html?scp=1&sq=Rene+Guim&st=nyt>

Rubin, Bob. "Cuba Relives Passion of U.S. Baseball Ties." The Miami Herald. 28 Mar. 1999.

Acknowledgements

First and foremost, I would like to thank Jason Browning for giving me the opportunity to be a part of this book. It's been a long road, but he has always been the stabilizing force and voice of reason behind this project. I hope his son, Colin, enjoys seeing his dad's name in print. I would also like to thank my family and friends, along with Jason's parents, who have been encouraging and supportive throughout. I would like to thank Michel and Marta Hernández for their continued interest in this project along with their insight. I would also like to thank everyone from my writer's group in Fort Smith for sharing their knowledge and experience. A *huge* 'thank you' goes out to Pam Pearce and Robbie Robertson for helping me pull everything together. Last, but most certainly not least, I would like to thank my two wonderful daughters, Lauren and Emily, who serve as constant inspiration.

About The Author

Clay McKinney is a native of Memphis and a graduate of the University of Tennessee, Knoxville. For the past eleven years, Clay and his wife and two daughters have resided in Fort Smith, Arkansas, where he continues to work on upcoming literary projects.

For more information, please visit:
www.pinstripedefection.com

www.ingramcontent.com/pod-product-compliance
Lightning Source LLC
Chambersburg PA
CBHW071957040426
42447CB00009B/1374